MARK SAVAGE

AUGUST KLEINZAHLER

Sallies, Romps, Portraits, and Send-Offs

August Kleinzahler was born in Jersey City, New Jersey, in 1949. He is the author of thirteen books of poems and a memoir, *Cutty, One Rock*. His collection *The Strange Hours Travelers Keep* was awarded the 2004 Griffin Poetry Prize, and *Sleeping It Off in Rapid City* won the 2008 National Book Critics Circle Award for poetry. That same year he received a Lannan Literary Award, and in 2017 he was awarded the Arthur Rense Poetry Prize by the American Academy of Arts and Letters. He lives in San Francisco.

Also by August Kleinzahler

SALLIES,

ROMPS,

PORTRAITS,

AND

SEND-OFFS

FARRAR

STRAUS

GIROUX

NEW

YORK

AUGUST

KLEINZAHLER

SALLIES,   SELECTED

ROMPS,   PROSE,

PORTRAITS,   2000-2016

AND

SEND-OFFS

Farrar, Straus and Giroux
175 Varick Street, New York 10014

Earlier versions of these essays originally appeared in the *London Review of Books*, *The San Diego Reader*, *The Threepenny Review*, *The Times Literary Supplement*, and the *Wildsam Field Guide* to San Francisco.

Grateful acknowledgment is made to the University of California Press for permission to reprint selections from *Lorine Niedecker: Collected Works*, by Lorine Niedecker, edited by Jenny Penberthy; © 2002 by the Regents of the University of California.

The Library of Congress has cataloged the hardcover edition as follows:
Names: Kleinzahler, August, author.
Title: Sallies, romps, portraits, and send-offs : selected prose, 2000–2016 / August Kleinzahler.
Description: First edition. | New York : Farrar, Straus and Giroux, 2017.
Identifiers: LCCN 2016041351 | ISBN 9780374282097 (hardcover)
Subjects: BISAC: LITERARY COLLECTIONS / Essays. | LITERARY CRITICISM / Poetry.
Classification: LCC PS3561.L38285 A6 2017 | DDC 814/.54—dc23
LC record available at https://lccn.loc.gov/2016041351

Paperback ISBN: 978-0-374-53767-8

Designed by Quemadura

Our books may be purchased in bulk for promotional, educational, or business use. Please contact your local bookseller or the Macmillan Corporate and Premium Sales Department at 1-800-221-7945, extension 5442, or by e-mail at MacmillanSpecialMarkets@macmillan.com.

www.fsgbooks.com
www.twitter.com/fsgbooks
www.facebook.com/fsgbooks

P1

FOR MARCELLE

The Boerum Hill bombshell

*Poetry is distinguished from prose by having
neither all the same restraints nor all the same
licenses. The essence of prose is to perish . . .*

—PAUL VALÉRY

*I do not believe that any distinction
between prose and poetry is meaningful.*

—T. S. ELIOT

CONTENTS

SALLIES,

ROMPS,

PORTRAITS,

AND

SEND-OFFS

FOG

Cold steamy air blew in through the open windows,
bringing with it half a dozen times a minute the
Alcatraz foghorn's dull moaning. A tinny alarm-clock,
insecurely mounted on a corner of Duke's Celebrated
Criminal Cases of America—*face down on the*
table—held its hands at five minutes past two.

DASHIELL HAMMETT,

THE MALTESE FALCON

The neighbor with the bad dog fiddles with her helmet and adjusts her front bicycle light before pushing off downhill in the fog. It is late for a bicycle ride, after ten p.m. Her dog throws himself against the glass of the front window behind the curtain, nearly strangling himself with snarls and a torturous medley of barks. She is headed west, in the direction of the ocean or park. There are dangers to be found this time of night in both places. But she is a fog chaser, and deepening night is best with the wind up and the cold, damp smoke blowing in off the sea at twenty knots. I can spot them, fog chasers, after so many years here. You might even say I'm such a one myself from time to time, especially when I find myself feeling more than a little *remote* from "society."

In the daylight hours, walking her vicious companion, occasionally bending over to pick up his stool with a small, white plastic baggie, one can see it in her eyes—the eyes of a fog chaser—haunted, darting about as if pursued by some threatening inner phantasm. She will rarely, if ever, engage the eyes of any stranger walking past, even as her creature takes a murderous lunge in his direction, gargling delirium at the end of his leash. But not mine—my eyes she will always look directly into, appraisingly and with a sneering displeasure. She knows that I know.

■

She saw it at a matinée toward the end of her last summer in Charleston, late July, before moving west to San Francisco. To escape the terrible heat and humidity, and just escape, she'd been attending quite a few matinées in that air-conditioned multiplex, those couple of weeks after she'd quit her job and before heading out.

We were standing at the bus stop, just across from what was then the Rock & Bowl at the foot of Haight Street, just twenty yards or so from the park, across Stanyan. It was late August, midafternoon. We could see the fog blowing in the way it does, along the ridge to the south of us, across Twin Peaks, Tank Hill, and the Sutro Forest behind the Medical Center.

She trembled. "You're cold," I said, wanting to put my arm around her but hesitating. We had only recently met, almost immediately after she arrived here by car, a long drive west with a friend. She was still rattled by it all: the drive, the breakup, the mess left behind—most everything, really. Presently, we would become lovers but not quite yet.

"No," she said, pausing a few moments. "I'm frightened." "Frightened?" I asked. "By what?" She seemed loath to say; embarrassed, I suppose. We said nothing for a minute or two. Then she said, "The fog." I was taken aback but didn't reply. Again she was quiet for some time. "You know, *The Fog*, that horror movie. I saw it back in Charleston at the matinée right before I left. "What happens with the fog in that movie?" I asked. "Nothing good," she said, turning to look me in the eyes, now clearly frightened and drawing close. "Nothing good."

■

It's way out there on the avenues, the north side of the park on Balboa, maybe a mile in from the ocean, hardly any other shops around, maybe a nondescript corner store or acupuncturist in the vicinity. It's a tiny place, with a big red sign above the glass front, SHANGHAI DUMPLING KING, with Chinese characters festooned all around the English like an aviary of tiny exotic birds.

It's bleak out there on the avenues this time of year, and gets bleaker still the closer you get to the water, and blowing. Nobody out on the street that doesn't have to be. There is a bus line that runs along here but only seldom. It's not a good part of town to be waiting for the bus, not at the back end of summer, I can tell you. You could compose half a sonnet sequence about the fog and wind and cold in your head while waiting for one to come by—that is if you're not stuck living out here in this god-forsaken part of town and happen to know the schedule by heart.

The windows of the restaurant are fogged up by the steam, either side of the glass. It's very quiet out there on the avenues, except for the low roar of wind, but inside, the restaurant is all noisy plate clatter, talk, busyness. It's always jam-packed.

Do you remember those warm spring twilights back east, playing Little League, the smell of hickory or white ash, cow-hide, grass, your cotton flannel uniform, the stands filled, and you coming to bat against Kenny Ray, the most feared pitcher in the league, big as a grown man and mean as hell, looking down at you from the mound with menace and contempt, the catcher behind you chattering away, saying nothing very encouraging? And somehow you get the head of your Louisville Slugger, the sweet spot, smack-dab on Kenny's fastball and drive it deep, deep to right center, all the way to the foot of the cyclone fence, deepest part of the outfield, crowd screaming, dugout screaming, Kenny looking like he just might jump right off the mound there and start chasing you down as you run the bases, probably throttle you to death.

Well, that's how they taste, the *xiaolongbao*, those Shanghai soup dumplings, when you bite into one of those plaited little darlin's, nippled at the top, the steamy-hot broth spurting into your mouth, bringing along with it the flavor of the pork, shrimp, and chives stuffed inside. And then you know, for sure, for dead-absolute certain, that in this cold, remorseless, fog-obliterated, windblown wretched old world, that somewhere out there, close on by the ocean, and if you know how to find it, there *is* this, *this*.

■

Steam rises from the wooden cistern. He unwraps the towels from my feet and begins digging deep into the tissue of my instep, working the Adrenals, Duodenum, and Hepatic Flexure. It is near the end of the day, Sunday, and the end of a long week. The fog, which never once burned off over the course of the day as it sometimes does this time of year, if only for an hour or two, has begun thickening, the Big Smoke Machine out there on the Pacific switching on as it always does at this hour, blowing in reinforcements down the flat, shop-lined corridor of Geary Boulevard.

There is some pain, occasionally sharp, as he probes deeper and deeper, exploring what time, misuse, and neglect have wrought upon my inner organs. He says nothing, and never looks up from his ministrations, grave faced, in total concentration, emitting only occasionally a muffled sound that rises from the base of his throat, suggesting perhaps some grim revelation, one best left unnamed and unspoken.

Presently, he moves to my toes, pinching and pulling,

raising—in his mind's eye—something like a primitive MRI or CAT scan image of my Pineal, Hypothalamus, and Axillary Lymphatics. But the pain he studiously inflicts, while holding fast to the methodical regimen and sequencing of his ancient art, is never, not at any single moment, entirely divorced from acute pleasure.

■

The bars have emptied, or begun emptying, today's ball game having recently concluded or the outcome seeming inevitable. It is early yet for the restaurants, but in some of the Chinese places families have already begun gathering for their early repast, and in others the kitchen staffs, likewise, sit around large tables and grab a quick meal before the dinner rush begins. The street is largely empty now. It is an in-between time, one of several in the course of the day, and when one turns a corner from one of the side streets onto Geary at this particular hour, the wind abruptly meets you and pushes you backward as if in a stern rebuke to never entirely let slip from your mind the record of all of history's misfortunes.

THOM GUNN

There's only one naked lady left, going to ruin out there in the fog amid the dahlias and lavender, its pink trumpet flowers wilted and in tatters. There used to be a couple of dozen of them blooming in the yard every August. Not much else was out there in the yard doing much of anything so the ladies made quite a spectacle of themselves, like Rockettes in a dusty frontier town. The neighbor on the third floor got a horticultural bee in his bonnet about seven years ago and dug the girls up, except the one. Of course, they weren't symmetrically arranged and, like some outlandish pink crepe accessory, didn't really go with anything else. But I hated to lose them. Like Paris, they looked their best in gray light.

Thom Gunn brought over a sackful of the bulbs (*Amaryllis belladonna*) I don't recall how many years ago, ten or twelve perhaps. He was always doing things like that. He liked gardening and wanted me to partake more fully of its pleasures. After his teaching obligations of the spring term at Berkeley ended every year, he would apply himself to his own small garden, sheltered and southeast facing. He seemed to enjoy organizing and cultivating his little patch of wild. And in this, as in most things, his approach was methodical, reasoned, and fastidious, even fussy.

Auden writes somewhere that it's good for a poet to have hobbies like gardening and cooking. This advice struck me as sound and I commend it to young writers. Thom, who was often compared to Auden on account of being queer, famous, and an English expatriate poet living in America, met Auden at least once. They didn't particularly get along. Thom wasn't at all catty about other poets (well, rarely), but at this late stage in his career Auden in public had become *Auden*. Thom remembered him going on at some length about martinis, what constituted a good one and where the best were to be found. This subject would have been of little or no interest to Thom then.

Thom admired Auden, at least his early poetry, which was a large influence on his own early work. Once, over lunch, he told the story of how Auden had come out here to San Francisco in 1954 and given a series of readings, the proceeds of which were handed over to the fledgling San Francisco State University Poetry Center in order to establish a reading series (a recent phenomenon popularized by Dylan Thomas) and archive. Auden stayed with Ruth Witt-Diamant, the Poetry Center's founding director, and, in return for his considerable largesse, asked only that he be delivered to gay bars where he might meet young Jewish American males with blond hair.

Thom Gunn arrived in the Bay Area that same year, following a young American Jewish male with blond hair, Mike Kitay, whom he had met and fallen in love with at Cambridge. Mike had been posted to San Antonio, Texas, to do his service in the U.S. Air Force. Thom took a steamship from England, stayed with Mike's family in New Jersey (who took him to Radio City Music Hall, where he probably saw the Rockettes), then moved on to California and took up studies with Yvor Winters at Stanford, an hour's drive south of San Francisco. He got a great deal from his time with Winters and wrote about it at length in what may be his finest essay, "On a Drying Hill: Yvor Winters."

He wore glasses and smoked a pipe, and both of these adjuncts served to mask a face that was not in any case volatile. Pleased or displeased, he was most of the time thoughtfully of the same expression; his shabby suit, too, always had the same unpressed demeanor. Almost any photograph taken of him in his last two decades shows accurately what he looked like. It was his voice that was remarkable, though I don't think I noticed it until I started taking his classes. He never played tricks with it, and in fact he habitually used a measured tone in conversation, but it was a voice which an actor would have envied, as you noticed as soon as he started to read poetry aloud. It was deep but capable of great variety in its modulation. It has always struck me that the argument of his essay on the audible reading of poetry is a little weakened by the fact that he could read poetry in what from anybody else would have been a monotone but from him was a controlled resonance, suggesting large emotions barely held in reserve.

Later on, after a not entirely comfortable year in San Antonio with Mike, teaching at the (then) very small Trinity College, Thom settled with him in the Bay Area. They remained together, with variations on the theme, for fifty years.

Thom liked to cook, as Auden also recommends, although almost certainly not on account of that recommendation. He wasn't a greatly gifted cook (he was, after all, an Englishman, and an Englishman of a particular generation), but he was more than passable: his pasta dishes were quite good, and he had a turkey recipe that involved cheesecloth, resulting in an uncommonly moist bird. As with his gardening, he was fastidious, methodical, and quietly determined, and a bit fussy: sober, spectacles resting on the tip of his nose, recipe book open at the appropriate page, stirring grimly away, eyes on the clock. I enjoyed many meals at his home. I remember one of my very first dinners there. Thom had asked me beforehand if there was anything I didn't eat. I responded as I always do: eggs, eel, and liver. Thom served me liver and bacon. He wasn't making a point, just absentminded. Cooking chores were rotated according to a predetermined schedule among the members of his household. Given certain lifestyle-related exigencies, this schedule was rather flexible, although negligence was registered and not without disfavor or recrimination.

Although we were good friends for twenty-three years, our friendship reached its apotheosis over the last few years of Thom's life, after his retirement from teaching, in our martini matinées. The word "matinée" has an old-fashioned, low meaning as an "afternoon tryst," but our martini matinées were only that: martinis at both ends of an afternoon movie. Don't get me wrong, Thom could be irrepressibly affectionate, especially after a couple of drinks. The first time he had me over to his place, he sat awfully close to me on his sofa in his tight jeans, sleeveless undershirt, and revolting tattoos, plying me with pot and wine. It was a bit of a worry for a moment or two. But I was, finally, not his type. And though he was a remarkably handsome sweetheart of a guy, not to mention a Faber poet, he sure as hell wasn't mine.

So all of that got sorted out from the get-go, and Thom was wonderfully kind to the women in my life, one after the other, and all of them adored him. He was a bit like a dream uncle: rather depraved, but endlessly decent, fun, generous, protective, encouraging, and abusive, cruel even, when he felt it warranted. But this was reserved almost exclusively for literary matters, when I'd written something he disapproved of. My writing has had no greater or more steadfast champion, but if he detected mannerism, slackness, want of real subject matter or its honest treatment, he let me have it with both barrels, sometimes firing below the belt. I didn't like it at the time, but it was a gift, really.

About me personally he seldom took issue. If I said something judgmental about someone, he'd give me a look. I was once walking down the street in Berkeley with another poet, quite famous, a truly reprehensible shit. He doesn't care for me either. We've just had a rather uncomfortable cup of coffee together, probably at Thom's suggestion, and this signature creep and I begin talking about Thom, a friend of both of ours, and the tenor of the conversation changes because we both love and revere Thom, and the creep starts telling a story the point of which is that Thom is the least judgmental person he's ever known. And I agree, not least because Thom puts up with this asshole. But it's true.

The only time Thom took issue with my extraliterary behavior was when I was having an illicit affair. His objection had nothing to do with sexual infidelity and the institution of marriage—how could it?—but he believed that over the course of such relationships one becomes accustomed to lying, and the habit of lying is detrimental to one's poetry.

Thom liked sex a great deal, sex and literature. He was consumed by both and consumed both in heroic proportions. He did his reading, and writing, in the mornings, and he prowled at night in the bars south of Market Street, an area that was known in the old days as South of the Slot, a bleak area of warehouses, small industry, and manufacturing. Nowadays the area is referred to in the tourist guides as SoMa and is a good deal more upscale and trendy. Had Thom lived another few years and got a book together, I think he intended to call it "South of the Slot."

I know more about Thom's literary enthusiasms than the other, but I know a little about the other. He spoke with unreserved and equal enthusiasm about both. I recall one afternoon when we were off on a reading tour together in Maryland and found ourselves in a mostly empty, rather genteel and expensive seafood restaurant out on the highway. The only other customers were a very elderly married couple, carefully attired in old people sporty formal, dourly and silently attending to their food. The two, clearly regulars, were an older version of the farm couple straight out of Grant Wood's *American Gothic*, transposed to the mid-Atlantic region. Thom, not at all charmed by the restaurant, and oblivious of the elderly couple, after several drinks launched into an extended graphic reprise of some pederastic debacle circa 1970. I was more than a little anxious that the oldsters might overhear his vivid rendering of events and drop dead from coronaries. But their closeness, my discomfort, and the emptiness of the dining room, not to mention the disappointing crab cakes and the prospect of a twenty-dollar cab fare back to the hotel, served only to encourage Thom's volubility, and the wine his volume.

I usually met with him for lunch at a pleasant restaurant on Cole Street, a three- or four-block walk for both of us. The martini matinées became an extension of these lunches. Apart from gossip, politics, what was doing in our lives, assorted mundanities, we mostly discussed what we were reading. Our lunches were by no means regular, and during the terms Thom was teaching, almost nonexistent. He tended to be cranky and inaccessible then. As with so much else, he was diligent and demanding of himself while lecturing. I often had a day job for seasons on end or was out of town for months at a time. After Thom's retirement, we got together on a more regular basis, say, once every two or three weeks.

The quality and acuity of his observations would startle me from time to time. If you know someone for a long time, you develop a sense of the way his mind works, his particular funds of knowledge, his intellectual propensities, and so forth. But Thom crossed me up any number of times. "Where the hell did that come from?" I'd think to myself. He wasn't at all a show-off. So many intellectuals, particularly university intellectuals, indulge in pissing contests over how much they've read, quoting at length by heart and so on. No wonder they have no friends off campus. Thom could more than hold his own if sucked into one or another of these contests, but it wasn't his sport. Apart from the bores and creeps, it was this brinksmanship, along with what Thom used to call, referring to London literary society, "the worst sort of village gossip," that put him off literary gatherings. It was a strong dislike we shared, among many other likes and dislikes.

Thom was vain of his good looks and sexual conquests but not of his poetry and learning. He knew the value of the latter and was not falsely modest, a trait he once told me he actively disliked in others.

Englishman that he was, however much he warred with the notion, Thom loved no authors more than Shakespeare and Dickens, and revisited both on pretty nearly an annual basis, usually over the summer when he had the most time. He liked picking up younger men and doing methamphetamine with them, and enjoyed bringing off a splendid poem of his own de-vising best of all—as you do if you're in that line of work—but he loved rereading Dickens and Shakespeare in his garden, al-ways finding new bits to marvel over. Not that he didn't stray to the Continent, also like the Englishman he was. He was mad for Stendhal, especially *The Charterhouse of Parma*, also Flaubert's *Sentimental Education*. Baudelaire's *Tableaux parisiens* meant quite as much to him as Donne or Marvell or Keats, all of whom meant a great deal. And at least one summer and fall were devoted to learning Italian, or just enough Italian, to get profitably through Dante in the original with the help of a crib. He wasn't big on poetry in translation.

I was a prime beneficiary of Thom's perspicacity over the years, but so were thousands of students at Berkeley over his forty years or so of teaching there. I tried to get him to allow me to sit in on his History of the English Lyric class one semester, but he said it would make him uncomfortable. My loss. I can't tell you how many books and authors he put me on to over the years. I could write a book . . . Actually, I did, or we did: an anthology of one hundred American poems. It was bravely commissioned by a trade publisher. (What in the world could they have been thinking?) Thom initially was chary of the project, worried that our friendship would suffer and that we would have to sift through the work of this and that celebrated no-talent in order to find a tolerable selection. But I impressed on him that we could put in or leave out whoever we bloody well liked. That reassured him, and we set to it in a leisurely fashion over many, many months. It went quite smoothly, really. We freely vetoed one another's choices, me with theatrical disgust, Thom with chilly contempt. We included a number of people who made our skin crawl, but Thom was more disciplined and fair-minded in this regard than I; besides which, that wasn't what it was about.

The publisher was horrified when he saw the list. "Where's Sylvia Plath? We haven't even heard of half these people!" The usual suspects, or most of them, were on board—Stevens, Eliot, Crane, Pound, Williams, there was even a poem of Lowell's— but not with their standard anthology pieces. About eighty percent of Thom's choices either had "Eros" in the title or were directly concerned with the troublesome deity. Nearly half the poets in the collection were women, but most of those we included you've probably never heard of. It was all terribly shocking.

Thom was a great reader of novels. He disdained short fiction and didn't read much nonfiction, unless it was Edward Gibbon or Darwin. I am nearly opposite in my tastes, but we did share our enthusiasms. Thom, for instance, thought Philip Roth was the cat's meow. I didn't. "Try *The Counterlife*," Thom said. Which I did, and it dazzled me.

Another time Thom said to me, "I've been reading Isaac Babel for the first time. He's very important to you, isn't he? Well, of course he is, he'd have to be." I gave Thom a copy of Charles Nicholl's *The Fruit Palace*, which he loved, likewise *Trainspotting*. Almost anything scatological had great appeal. He also enjoyed the Richard Yates books I shared with him. When I was ill at one point, I read through all of Derek Raymond, whom I recommend to anyone with a stubborn bacterial infection. "Oh, yes," Thom said, "he's wonderful, isn't he." Sometimes we came on an author separately that sent us both head over heels. I don't recall who got there first, or how, but at one point we were both roaring through the novels of James Buchan, and when we sat down to lunch together we could barely contain our enthusiasm, like a couple of teenage girls gushing about a cute new boy at school.

During our final lunch, the Thursday before the Sunday he died, we discussed the anthology ("They'll never do it," Thom said) and J. R. Ackerley, the last among the scores of writers I'd never have found had it not been for Thom. "His writing is close in style to Isherwood's," I said to Thom. "Who was influenced by whom?"

"Oh, Ackerley by Isherwood, certainly," he said. "Ackerley didn't do most of his good writing until later in life, long after he'd been a friend of Isherwood's and an admirer of his writing."

After lunch I dropped Thom off at the cheese shop where he always got his pesto and grated pecorino. He was nothing if not regular in his habits: the tea shop on Haight Street, the Alpha Market for plonk and cuts of meat, the Hole in the Wall for sex.

There wasn't much going on in April in the way of movies, so we were strapped, at least so far as our martini matinée routine. I was headed off for a few weeks. We agreed that surely there would be something worth seeing on my return. Our partings, even if for extended periods of time, were never occasions for much physical display. I don't think that Thom really liked being touched very much unless sexually. Shaking hands seemed to confuse and mildly upset him. I'm not terribly comfortable kissing other males. I think what it came to over the years was, on my part, a rather martial tug and squeeze of his shoulder, followed by a partial hug. That seemed to go down okay, and it went down okay that last time. I don't believe either of us thought it would be the last time.

What I remember, and will remember, most vividly about our friendship was traveling around town with Thom on public transport. Neither of us had cars. We were more often than not heading to a movie, and the prospect and the adventure of getting to the cinema seemed to put Thom in high spirits. To travel with Thom was to participate in an erotic mapping of San Francisco out the bus window. I was reminded of the early Renaissance maps in which significant sites like the cathedral or castle are wildly out of proportion, or the Mappa Mundi in which Jerusalem, say, is placed at the center of the world and given space equivalent to its spiritual or political importance, not its actual physical size and geographical situation.

For Thom, the city seemed to exist as a complex of erotic sites, assignations, stews. Heterosexual males, in my experience, are without exception tedious and irritating, not to mention unreliable, on this subject. But Thom, on passing a bar or apartment or street corner (in one memorable instance a phone booth in a rather tony part of town), seemed cheerful and nostalgic in equal measure, and almost always had an amusing or interesting anecdote. If one or two sites or parts of the city defied scale on Thom's map in the way the cathedral and castle did in old maps, they would probably be the Stud and the Hole in the Wall, and his Jerusalem would be South of the Slot.

I don't recall when our martini matinées began, exactly. We

would have been early for a movie and found ourselves a bar. I am not ordinarily an afternoon drinker, but when I drink I prefer spirits, and like many other drinkers in middle age I have, for the most part, moved from brown-colored spirits to the less punitive clear. My ordinary drink out these days is a Ketel One martini, up with a twist, very dry.

Thom was a wine drinker and enjoyed a couple of glasses of plonk over lunch. But he seemed to enjoy doing as I did when we were together at a bar, as well as liking the knowledgeable sound of my order. So he, too, had a martini, the same as mine. Martinis, as Auden would attest, pack a wallop. Thom banged back his martini, checked his watch, and seeing we had all of five minutes left till showtime, ordered a second round.

He tended to be exuberant under the influence of alcohol and quite uninhibited. Even when sober he had an enormous laugh, one that would often turn heads in public places. One time we caught a matinée of *Sexy Beast*, and after the movie, and after a couple of postmovie martinis that had become over time part of the ritual, we got caught up in a "you fucking cunt" jag. This continued beyond the movie theater and bar (the very unprepossessing Hockey Haven), to the bus, and then, having to change buses, at the bus stop on Masonic and Geary where we horrified some perfectly nice old Chinese people, then on the next bus, filled with people returning home from work and students from high school. "You fucking cunt." "Who's a fucking cunt, you fucking cunt?" and so forth. The spectacle would have been obnoxious enough if the dickheads involved were fourteen-year-olds, but in this case one of them was seventy-two and regarded as one of the most important poets in the English language, and the other dickhead, though a good deal younger, was not at all young.

Thom's mother killed herself when he was a boy. Any child would be terribly affected by this, I realize, but I think they were especially close. After his mother's death, reading and books became his world; even as an adult he tended to view the world and people through the filter of literature. It's evident in the poetry. Thom's mother had a good friend named Thérèse. Although his aunts took him in after the suicide and looked after him, he sometimes stayed with Thérèse, who had a son his age. I forget exactly what Thom told me about her—sophisticated, arty, Jewish, somehow involved with the theater, a good friend of Peggy Ashcroft. What Thom especially liked about Thérèse was that she treated him as an adult and confided in him, more so than in her own son. I remember in the last year or two of his life Thom talking about a great snow in the winter of 1947, a snow such as London had never seen. It had been an unusually cold winter, a legendary winter. Thom was staying at Thérèse's; it was a weekend or holiday morning, perhaps even Christmas. When he awoke the city was covered in white, an amazing spectacle, everything come to a halt, nothing but white. I could tell by Thom's expression while recounting the episode that he was, at that particular moment, having pulled back the curtains on that particular morning so many years before, perfectly happy.

LIVING ON APPLE CRUMBLE

James Schuyler's Letters

"I am well. How are you? It is wonderful here," the first letter in *Just the Thing: Selected Letters of James Schuyler* begins, and goes on: "I love it here; real mad fun. Especially the evening game of gin rummy before beddy-by (9:30); the 8 p.m. cup of cocoa." The letter was written on November 15, 1951, a few days after James Schuyler had been admitted to Bloomingdale Hospital, a mental institution in White Plains, New York. Schuyler still gets his semicolons right, and his appetite for gossip is undiminished: "Is it still Connecticut, the dear deer, the steady lay, the unprivate walls?" His correspondent, John Hohnsbeen, an art-dealer friend, was having an affair with the architect Philip Johnson, and the "unprivate walls" are those of Johnson's famous Glass House.

Schuyler was twenty-eight and this was his first serious mental breakdown. He had only recently arrived in New York after an extended stay in Italy, where he worked for a time as Auden's secretary in Ischia, typing up, among other things, the poems that became the collection *Nones*. Schuyler later claimed that working for Auden made him think: "Well, if this is poetry, I'm certainly not going to write any myself." But over the next twenty-five years or so, he produced some of the most brilliant and distinctive poetry written in English in the second half of the last century, as well as a remarkable novella masquerading as a children's book, *Alfred and Guinevere*, and a body of art criticism, mostly written for *ARTnews*, which contains some of the most perceptive commentary on the downtown Manhattan art scene of his time.

Through the poet-friendly Tibor de Nagy Gallery, which opened in a cold-water flat on East 52nd Street in 1950, the year before Schuyler's breakdown, Schuyler met John Ashbery, Kenneth Koch, and Frank O'Hara, who had been friends at Harvard. The "Harvard wits," he called them. Schuyler had attended Bethany College, a small school in West Virginia affiliated with the Disciples of Christ, where he had devoted himself to bridge rather than his studies and so flunked out.

The four poets became known as the New York School, a tag thought up by the gallery's director, John Myers, who was described by James Merrill as "an ageless, hulking Irishman with the self-image of a pixie." They certainly didn't consider themselves a "school," but they were smart and talented, as were the painters associated with the gallery: Willem de Kooning, Jackson Pollock, Philip Guston, Mark Rothko, Helen Frankenthaler, Jane Freilicher, Grace Hartigan, Alfred Leslie, Larry Rivers, Norman Bluhm, and Fairfield Porter. It all made for a vigorous little scene, a fair bit of it played out at the Cedar Bar, then on 9th Street in Greenwich Village, where, as O'Hara would later write, "we often wrote poems while listening to the painters argue and gossip." It's a world generously chronicled, and in the most informal of ways, in this very ample and entertaining collection of Schuyler's letters.

Auden and his crowd had provided Schuyler with his entrée into the world of serious artists. About Auden himself, Schuyler had mixed feelings. He wrote an affectionate, not very good elegy, "Wystan Auden," which appears in his 1980 collection *The Morning of the Poem*, for which he won the Pulitzer Prize. He deserved a Pulitzer many times over for his first two collections, *Freely Espousing* (1969) and *The Crystal Lithium* (1972), but the collection with the Auden elegy in it isn't much good. The years of Milltown, Nembutal, Thorazine, lithium, and the rest had coarsened Schuyler's matchlessly delicate touch.

Schuyler wasn't too keen on Auden's later work. "It is *The Old Man's Road* you are reviewing, isn't it?" he wrote to Kenneth Koch in January 1957:

I read some of it and dropped it with a little whinny of disgust. He really is a pig. Well, now let's see. First, he wrote the poems at the end . . . of his self-exile in "Amedica." He has the chair of poetry at Oxford, his bally old university . . . Well, he has always been envious of Eliot, and if *The Old Man's Road* is no *4 Quartets* it may be, in a nasty sort of way, his *Ash Wednesday* (why should the aged beagle stretch its legs, he yawned, scratching himself with his singing bone) . . . The poems are probably also the expression of a periodic self-disgust (another instance is the kind of mutilation that got into his *Collected Poems*: putting camp titles on serious poems; tearing apart *The Orators*; ripping choruses out of plays he has written with

Isherwood . . .). Now, you like his early work. Isherwood had a great deal to do with it: he criticized his poems, cut them to pieces and so on. It's all in *Lions & Shadows*. But as the boy grew older, there wasn't anybody bright enough to keep up with him . . . And he has little faculty for self-criticism (which is a quality—if it is worth anything—one might expect a poet, an artist, to develop rather than possess innately).

While Schuyler and his circle tolerated Auden, Robert Lowell and his reputation gave them fits. Schuyler would define his poetic project, at least in part, by opposing it to that of Lowell and the other gloomy campus darlings of the New Critics:

New York poets, except I suppose the color-blind, are affected most by floods of paint in whose crashing surf we all scramble.

Artists of any genre are of course drawn to the dominant art movement in the place where they live; in New York it is painting. Not to get mixed up in it would be a kind of blinders-on repression, like the campus dry-heads who wishfully descend tum-ti-tumming from Yeats out of Graves with a big kiss for Mother England (subject of a famous Böcklin painting: just when did the last major English poet die? not that Rossetti isn't fun . . .). The big thing happening at home is a nuisance, a publicity plot, a cabal; and please don't track the carpet.

A letter to Donald Allen in September 1959 lists his influences, and those of his New York pals. These include Auden ("though if Auden doesn't drop that word numinous pretty soon, I shall squawk"), Pound, Eliot, and Marianne Moore (but "after a bout of syllable counting, to pick up D. H. Lawrence is delightful"), Stevens and William Carlos Williams ("both inspire greater freedom than the others, Stevens of the imagination, Williams of subject and style"). Then Schuyler says that "Continental European literature is, really, the big influence," mentioning, among others, Reverdy, Max Jacob, Breton, Supervielle, Apollinaire, and, somewhat surprisingly, Pasternak, who "has meant more to us than any American poet. Even in monstrous translations his lyrics make the hair on the back of one's neck curl."

The "monstrous translations" may well be those of Lowell, in his collection of loose renderings, *Imitations*. It's unclear what excites Schuyler about Pasternak, or at least what influence Pasternak had on his poetry. There are certainly affinities between the poetry of Pasternak and Lowell, but Schuyler and his friends have intractable problems with the seriousness of Lowell, which they find unconvincing, while they are moved by Pasternak, particularly by his elegy for Anna Akhmatova, which Lowell translates:

> The dry wind dances like a dried-out walnut
> across the waves, across your stung eyelids—
> stars, branches, milestones, lamps. A white
> seamstress on the bridge is always washing clothes.

> I know that objects and eyesight vary greatly
> in singleness and sharpness, but the iron
> heart's vodka is the sky
> under the northern lights.

Perhaps the New York poets admired Pasternak's invisibility.

Schuyler, O'Hara, Ashbery, and Koch all have difficulty with seriousness. It is a difficulty that, when they engage with it, creates the most interesting tension in their work. These four poets insist on a tone of offhandedness, a casualness which, when it hardens into mannerism, as it often does, is no less obnoxious than Lowell's straining after the transcendently poetic, as in "Skunk Hour":

> I watched for love-cars. Lights turned down,
> they lay together, hull to hull,
> where the graveyard shelves on the town . . .
> My mind's not right.
>
> A car radio bleats,
> "Love, O careless Love . . ." I hear
> my ill-spirit sob in each blood cell,
> as if my hand were at its throat . . .
> I myself am hell,
> nobody's here—
>
> only skunks . . .

This poem would set O'Hara off:

I don't think that anyone has to get themselves to go and watch lovers in a parking lot necking in order to write a poem, and I don't see why it's admirable if they feel guilty about it. They should feel guilty. Why are they snooping? What's so wonderful about a Peeping Tom? And then if you liken them to skunks putting their noses into garbage pails, you've just done something perfectly revolting. No matter what the metrics are.

O'Hara and Schuyler shared an apartment on and off from 1952 until the beginning of 1957. Never lovers, they had a very close, quite difficult relationship. O'Hara was an electric presence, the straw that stirred the drink in whatever social situation he found himself. Schuyler was no less ambitious but was quite happy to let others lobby on behalf of his genius, and they did. There were jealousies and suspicion, at least on Schuyler's part. Here is a 1957 letter about their relationship from O'Hara to Ashbery, which appears in David Lehman's useful *The Last Avant-Garde* (1998):

> I don't see any use in either of us going through the strain of pretending we like each other as much as we once did. I don't know why, for instance, he has singled me out for the accusation that I've put him in the shade as a writer, or whatever he said, except that I have been more handy than you or Kenneth . . . but he apparently wants to blame it on me for allegedly damaging his self-confidence, so that's the way it is.

O'Hara and Schuyler finally fell out in 1961, not long after Schuyler had to be admitted to a mental hospital again. When

O'Hara died in 1966, Schuyler was shaken, although it's not terribly evident in the letter he wrote to Ashbery three days later:

> I still feel stunned by Frank's death. If you feel equal to it, I would like to know a little more than is in today's *Times*: who he was staying with? Or anything you think I might want to know. But if you would rather not write about it don't . . .
>
> It was like a dream come true to have you here, and unfortunately as quickly passed. Joe [Brainard] writes that "you got some dishes"—what are they like? Also, how long does the bus trip from Vermont (Burlington?) take?

Schuyler wrote two poems in memory of O'Hara, the first a stunner titled "Buried at Springs"; the other, "To Frank O'Hara," from his 1974 book *Hymn to Life*, was written after his style had turned wooden. The earlier poem begins:

> There is a hornet in the room
> and one of us will have to go
> out the window into the late
> August midafternoon sun. I
> won . . .

The poem describes a summer's day at Fairfield Porter's summerhouse on Great Spruce Island in Penobscot Bay, Maine, which O'Hara visited a number of times. The poem mentions O'Hara briefly, sitting at the desk where Schuyler is now writing the poem, [O'Hara] taking in the sounds of the water, the crickets, looking out at the spruce, the "new seaweed / on the low-tide rocks." It is "a day," Schuyler writes, "subtle and suppressed / in mounds of juniper enfolding / scratchy pockets of shadow." The poem concludes:

> Delicate day, setting the bright
> of a young spruce against the cold
> of an old one hung with unripe cones
> each exuding at its tip
> gum, pungent, clear as a tear,
> a day tarnished and fractured
> as the quartz in the rocks
> of a dulled and distant point,
> a day like a gull passing
> with a slow flapping of wings
> in a kind of lope, without
> breeze enough to shake loose
> the last of the fireweed flowers,
> a faintly clammy day, like wet silk
> stained by one dead branch
> the harsh russet of dried blood.

Robert Lowell also had a summer home on Penobscot Bay, in the village of Castine. "Skunk Hour" takes place there. It's worth comparing the tone and method of Schuyler's elegy for O'Hara with Lowell's poem "For John Berryman":

> I feel I know what you have worked through, you
> know what I have worked through—we are words . . .

> John, we used the language as if we made it.
> Luck threw up the coin, and the plot swallowed,
> monster yawning for its mess of potage.

Lowell memorializes his friend by pitching the diction toward the heroic; Schuyler, as he so often does, locates his emotion in a landscape, finding something like an "objective correlative" there, resistant as he would have been to the term.

There is only one letter to O'Hara in *Just the Thing*, and it is addressed not only to him but also to the painter John Button, object of Schuyler's affection at the time. The O'Hara estate promised to provide the Schuyler letters but failed to deliver them. I wonder how much they would add to this book. Here's part of the one letter there is, written by Schuyler from Fairfield Porter's home in Southampton on Long Island in the summer of 1956:

> Dear "John" and "Frank,"
>
> (Or shouldn't I call you by your camp names in a letter.)
>
> I loved your antiphonal psalm—it was like getting a jeweler's box with a sparrow in it that had been fucked to death by John Simon . . . So I thought I'd let Schiz and Oid, the two halves of my personality, collaborate and bake you both a plate of my favorite cakes. ("Take one krater of goat piss and crumble in it enough camel dung to make a workable paste. Pat into cakes and put aside to rest. When an iridescent sheen like that in the eye of a peacock feather appears, bake the cakes in a fast oven, garnish with rabbit berries and serve hot in a napkin.

These tasty morsels are the Quiffquiff spoken of so highly by Lawrence of Arabia . . .")

    My, we really are just like the Brontë sisters . . .

    So you've seen some movies have you, you rats. Out here they are following up *The Catered Affair*, which I drew my tiny line at, with *Diabolique* . . .

The letter ends:

Well, Sieve-lips and Paddle-tongue, I sure hope for all our sakes that this doesn't fall into the hands of the Feds!

    Love from yo' ol' Mammy,

    Jimminey Yuk-Yuk

Depending on your appetite for camp, reading the Schuyler letters from beginning to end may make you feel as though you've been living on apple crumble for a week. Apple crumble of a very high order, but apple crumble nevertheless. His many letters to Ashbery, for instance, are addressed to alter egos, such as "Kewpie," "Blackie Cinders," "Grinling Gibbons," "Purvis," "Regency Rake," "Painless Parker," "Tempest Storm," "Beany Bacon Dip," "Rich Freeze-Dried Coffee Chunks," and "Piccolo Pete." The letters themselves, both to Ashbery and Koch, though they leak generously with keen observations, literary, artistic, personal, and otherwise, chiefly document the social comings and goings of the very busy, fizzy gay end of the very busy, fizzy New York art world of the 1950s. In fact, it would be impossible to get through this volume without a program guide, such are the couplings, B movies, art openings, concerts, fallings-out, parties, bon mots, weekends in the country, etc. The editor, William Corbett, who spent thirteen years putting this collection together, has provided an admirable equivalent in his extensive footnotes, glossary, and index, along with a sharp introduction.

The best letters, for my money, are to the less central characters in Schuyler's life, or the more ephemeral ones. His attitude toward letter writing is obliquely described in a letter to John Button from May 4, 1956:

> The first use of drawings is the same as that of notebooks and letters for a writer: practice and keeping your hand in it: Kyriena [Siloti]'s finger exercises. So if I object to titles, it's merely that it verges toward an attitude of which Gide is such a perfectly sad example, keeping your diary for the public; it might imply that one had had a preconceived idea in the back of one's mind, that when one was most private one had, to a small degree, limited one's perfect freedom.

This is part of a long, revealing letter that is far more interesting than most any of the letters to Ashbery and Koch. Schuyler goes on:

> About your drawings: I rather question the kind of drawing paper you use: it somewhat resembles photographic paper, and its gloss tends to kill the lightness of a line made with hard graphite. When smudged, it gives a very pretty atmo-

spheric tone, but one which seems more inherent in the paper and graphite than something put there. I find it, in a word, impersonal.

There is a line you sometimes use in your drawings which is stunning because of its speed, but which does not always tell as much as it appears to: if it's undesirable, it's because it gives off a look of "finish," and a work should not look more finished than it intrinsically is . . . A deeper trouble with the speedy kind of line I mean is that one important reason for making drawings, I imagine, is not to draw a likeness of what one sees but to find out what it is one sees.

The artist who also writes criticism, whether about his own art or someone else's, will, inevitably, tell you what he himself is up to, or at least aspires to. Praising a work by Fairfield Porter, Schuyler writes: "The most forceful quality of this particular painting is the artist's willingness to be clumsy." Of all the letters here, those to Porter, the first dated Bastille Day 1954, and the last August 9, 1972, are the clumsiest and most interesting. In them Schuyler casts about, struggling to find a register in which to engage the older artist:

And while I'm at it, I'm also rather put out by this youth and age stuff. In so far as I think of you as "older," I feel honored and benefited by your friendship; but if it turns out that you feel odd in bestowing it, I feel snubbed. I don't, though, think of you as "older" so much as I do a friend who has had a life very different from mine (but if I must think about it, then I

say that I think I'm a man over thirty, past which age one might
hope to have gained the right to mingle with one's elders &/or
betters).

Schuyler's finest poems, with the exception of the long poem
"The Crystal Lithium," are landscapes and interiors, paintings
in language, and quite unlike the poetry of O'Hara, Ashbery,
and Koch, or anyone else who comes to mind, apart from his
epigones. When asked once if he had ever written any poems
about Porter's paintings, Schuyler replied that he hadn't but that
he'd written a number of poems *like* Porter's paintings. "Going,"
from *Freely Espousing*, is a good example. It begins:

> In the month when the Kamchatka bugbane
> finally turns its strung-out hard pellets white
> and a sudden drench flattens the fugitive
> meadow saffron to tissue-paper scraps
> and winds follow that crack and bend without breaking
> the woody stems of the chrysanthemums so the good of not
>   disbudding
> shows in lower smaller flights of metallic pungency,
> a clear zenith looks lightly dusted and fades to nothing
> at the skyline, shadows float up to lighted surfaces
> as though they and only they kept on the leaves
> that hide their color in a glassy shine.

Later we move to an interior:

> . . . early, in the middle
> of the afternoon, the light slants

into rooms that face southwest: into this room
across a bookcase so the dead-brown gold-stamped
spines look to be those to take down now:
Hodge and His Masters, The Cereals in America.
If a leaf of gold were beaten to transparency
and all that here roots and extrudes were tarnished silver
and blackened bronze—bumped and brushed against
here and there into high lights—
were seen through it by the wind-flickered quick-setting sun,
October would look no different than it looks.

This poem was almost certainly written at the Porters' house in Southampton, where Schuyler was not only a regular guest but also for a time a member of the family with his own room. Anne Porter, Fairfield's wife, said that Schuyler came "for a weekend and stayed 11 years."

As a figurative painter, Porter would seem to have been the odd man out among the Abstract Expressionists associated with the Tibor de Nagy Gallery. But de Kooning and the others revered him because of the way he handled abstract elements in his landscapes and domestic interiors. Porter once said, according to Schuyler, that "'the right use of color can make *any* composition work,' and that in fact color *is* the composition." Schuyler's principal interest as a poet was color and light, and he paid attention to the weather and the landscape, transforming the ordinary and everyday into something luminous and enduring, but without inflating his subject matter: he was determined not to poeticize the material. In a piece about Porter in the journal *Arts* in 1976, Louis Finkelstein wrote: "Subject-matter must be normal in the sense that it does not appear sought after so much as simply happening to one." This sums up Schuyler's poetry, too.

Fairfield Porter died suddenly in 1975, the one person, Schuyler maintained, who had never let him down. By this point, Schuyler had moved out of the Porters' house and was drifting around New York from rooming house to nursing home to psychiatric hospital, more or less living off the kindness of friends, finally settling at the Chelsea Hotel in 1979. When asked by *The Village Voice* why he lived there, Schuyler wrote:

> When I was twenty I came to New York because it was the center, I guess. I was coming from west New York State, a place called East Aurora. It's still the center. I stay because I have friends here. I suppose I'd really rather live in the country, but I can't afford a house, so I live in the Chelsea. It's comfortable here and I have a balcony and it's convenient. Convenient to what? John Ashbery.

James Schuyler died of a stroke at the Chelsea in April 1991. There's a plaque by the hotel entrance with his name on it.

LEONARD MICHAELS

Lenny Michaels was the kind of Jew I particularly like: a "throw-back" to an earlier era is how he was described in his *New York Times* obituary. He was a *k'nocker*, a big shot, a wise guy, but a *k'nocker* who delivered. There's a big difference. He was a *where's the action / I'm up to it* sort of Yid. Lenny was the anti–Woody Allen.

Lenny talked; you listened. That's how it was with Lenny. Which would ordinarily be obnoxious or boring, but not with Lenny. It was big fun to be ranted at by Lenny. Even if he was talking bushwa and bravado, it never seemed bushwa and bravado at the time. It was all about his schemes, the bloody battles to be waged for art or glory or money, usually all three. And, of course, it was about Lenny.

I first met Leonard Michaels—or, rather, was accosted by him—at a poetry reading I gave at Berkeley thirty years ago. How, you might ask, is one accosted at a poetry reading? A fair question. Well, I gave the reading. Lenny liked it. But Lenny didn't do merely *like*, he *extravagated.* He seemed to be beside himself, poking his finger in my chest, telling me what I was, what I had done—in this instance, a writer, a poet, who had pleased him inordinately.

What's this skinny old guy with outrageous '70s sideburns poking me for? I mean, who the fuck is this person? He didn't look like a professor, not one bit. He certainly didn't act like a professor. A pretty young woman, my age at the time, stood two paces behind Lenny, presumably his consort. She was smiling politely, mildly embarrassed by Lenny, almost certainly not for the first time, or last.

I had come directly from my job at the lock shop that evening. I don't know that I even had the opportunity to change. Maybe Caroline threw a sports jacket in the back of her car. It would have been Thom Gunn who invited me. No one else would have thought to, not before or since. Before the reading Thom asked me solicitously, "Augie, do you need to make wee-wee beforehand?" That was Thom . . . There would likely have been another reader, probably some pill of a graduate student, a devoted acolyte of this creative writing instructor or that, who wrote in the manner of his instructor but less distinctively or well, so as to remain unthreatening.

I do remember that Lenny absolutely *loved* the idea that I worked in a lock shop; in fact, he borrowed a book of mine about locksmithing that he never returned. That's okay; somehow I wasn't too optimistic about ever getting it back. I was already experienced enough to know that fiction writers are always on the prowl for goodies, for anything out of the ordinary that might be dished out down the road, that might serve to garnish a tale—and I knew that Lenny would, someday, all of a sudden, be in need of a locksmith or some locksmithing lore.

If you want my advice, don't go on a date with a story writer, and certainly don't go on a second date.

■

Lenny was in a heat to get together with me. We met a couple of weeks later at Brennan's, a barn of a place just off the University exit on 580. It was a steam-table-cum-bar affair, the sort of place workingmen and bachelors went: impersonal, functional, but not unpleasant. Its most distinctive feature was that it could not have been more un-Berkeley. We might as well have been in Cleveland. Lenny gave the initial impression we were involved here in something vaguely illicit, an intrigue.

But that was Lenny: he dwelt in the atmosphere of perpetual vexation. It was part of his appeal. That evening, which I still remember vividly, Lenny talked, I drank. What flowed from him was a monologue about his adventures, frustrations, amours, ailments, his storied basketball career at NYU, the condition of the Jew in the universe, mambo lessons, vendettas, of which he had not a few going, movie scripts, movies, movie directors, movie producers, movie dolls—he was gone on the idea of movies and he coveted the prospect of his becoming a sort of super-duper, highbrow Robert Towne.

Lenny was a great talker, very expressive. Not all good writers are good talkers—in fact, most of the ones I've met strike me as autistic to varying degrees—but Lenny was spellbinding. He seemed able to bring his literary gifts of description, pacing, narrative, and portraiture to the realm of conversation. His method of engaging you was to give the impression he was taking you into his confidence, sharing urgent insights and intimacies for no other reason than that he trusted your unique intelligence, insight, and judgment. He would interrupt his stream of talk periodically and look furtively around the room, lest someone else be listening in.

Of course, by this stage I had read his two early short story collections and his novel *The Men's Club*, and knew what he was worth as a writer. The novel was racy and smart but conceived as a movie down the road (a prospect never far from Lenny's mind—a movie that got made and bombed), but the stories were terrific, beautifully put together, sentence by sentence, with no small measure of psychological savagery, generating serious heat. Lenny at his best was the kind of prose writer a poet who weighs every word, who puts phrases and sentences together syllable by syllable, turning each element over in his mind, can really dig into with pleasure. I can tell all I need to know about a writer's prose before I'm halfway through the first paragraph, and I was gone on Lenny's writing by the third sentence. Naturally, I was flattered and excited, still a young and conspicuously unsuccessful writer, to be sharing an evening with this brilliantly engaging meshuggener, to be spoken to as an equal. I remember Caroline asking me later that evening, after I'd driven home, "What's gotten into *you*?"

And that was that. We'd bump into one another over the years: he'd be smoking up a storm, kvetching about an underappreciated film script he'd written or about some imaginary ailment. "Hey, I've got to get that book back to you, the one about locks," he'd say. We were always glad to see one another. Of course, Lenny was twenty years my senior and on a different plane so far as success in this world, but Lenny was also infatuated with glamour, clout, Hollywood. He wanted to be the intellectual who broke through into the larger popular culture. He'd already gotten plenty, but there was no end to how much more lay out there for him to plunder, if only those *stupid fucking bastards would come to their senses*. Me, he regarded, I think, as an amiable, dreamy sort of schlep, but he liked my poetry and I liked his stories, which is as good a bond as most; in hindsight, probably better than most.

Another couple of years went by and then, one Friday night, I received a frantic call from Lenny. I had to help him. It was urgent, a huge favor. I had to read something of his. Only I would really know if it was any good. Only I could be trusted to tell him the truth. He was as full of intrigue and melodrama as ever. He was already in San Francisco, not far. I told him to come by.

It was the tail end of a dinner party when Lenny arrived in a state of extreme agitation, ignoring those present, including a very young woman, still a coed, who would eventually become

Lenny's friend as well as his editor, publishing the "Nachmann" stories at *The New Yorker*, and who would, thirteen years later, in 2003, be quoted about Lenny in his *Times* obituary. But Lenny was in a heat and oblivious at the time. He wasn't being rude; he was being Lenny. I had to read his new manuscript over the next thirty-six hours and report to him at lunch that Sunday, like I had nothing better to do. Only I could help him. *Me.* Of course, I didn't believe him for an instant and felt certain he'd already showed the book to a dozen others, but was flattered, regardless. Also, reading anything of Lenny's, no matter how ephemeral, gave me pleasure.

I neither had nor have any special knowledge of prose fiction. In fact, I had and have little time for most fiction. Lenny's fiction I did have time for. But I could tell straightaway that Lenny was rushing a book into print that wasn't nearly ready. To this day I don't know why. The collection was anchored by his most brilliant short story, "Sylvia," which he had extended to almost novella length, about a mentally unstable former girlfriend, then wife, and the Greenwich Village scene of the early '60s. It sat amid the rest of the collection like a huge, incandescent meteorite in a field of granite boulders. What was I to say to him, this brilliant, flamboyant, older writer with his enormous reputation, his soft Italian leather boots, his sports car, his beautiful wives, his tsuris with Hollywood producers, those "stupid schmucks"? What was I to tell Leonard Michaels? "Lenny, you don't have a book here"?

Lenny was very grateful, and eager to take me to a swank restaurant for lunch as my reward. Me, I'm a schlep. I liked the ginger salad at a Burmese restaurant just across town, a linoleum and Formica joint over on California in the Richmond district.

Lenny said with dismay, "A Burmese restaurant?"

"You'll like it, Lenny, trust me, you'll see. They do a good job, best in town."

Lenny took me for ginger salad.

"So?" he said.

"Lenny," I said, "you're a brilliant writer. You know better than anyone what should go in, what should go where, what shouldn't. *You*, in your heart," I said, "*you*, Lenny, *you*, only *you* know best."

Lenny looked at me with incredulity. I cringed.

"That's the most amazing piece of advice anyone has ever given me, ever!" Lenny said. I had never seen Lenny so delighted or triumphant.

The book was savaged in *The New York Times Book Review* by Anatole Broyard, two whole pages. I've never read such a review, before or since. Lenny must have screwed one of Broyard's girlfriends. He was so exercised by Lenny in general that he didn't even get to Lenny's book until the last paragraph, so busy was he pissing from a great height on Lenny and his *inflated* reputation.

I still have the inscribed copy of the book Lenny gave me:

To August,
Who did
More than he
    Knows to
    Shape this
    Book. With
    Gratitude.
                Lenny   1991

ALL THE GIRLS SAID SO

John Berryman

As John Berryman tells it, in a *Paris Review* interview conducted in 1970, he was walking to a bar in Minneapolis one
evening in the mid-1950s with his second wife, Ann, the two of
them joking back and forth, when Berryman volunteered that
he "hated the name Mabel more than any other female name."
Ann decided Henry was the name she found "unbearable." For
a long time afterward, "in the most cozy and affectionate lover
kind of talk . . . she was Mabel and I was Henry." Not long after
that, Berryman began to write his Dream Songs with a song he
later "killed":

> The jolly old man is a silly old dumb
> with a mean face, humped, who kills dead.
> There is a tall who loves only him.
> She has sworn "Blue to you forever,
> Gray to the little rat, go to bed."
> I fink it's bads all over.

It ends:

> Henry and Mabel ought to but can't.
> Childness let's have us honey—

"It set the prosodic pattern," Berryman told the interviewer, Peter Stitt, who had been a student of his a few years earlier. The interview was conducted in a ward in St. Mary's Hospital in Minneapolis, where Berryman seemed to be comfortable. He spent quite a bit of time there during the last few years of his life. In January 1972 he jumped to his death from a nearby bridge.

That "prosodic pattern" would evolve into one of the significant poetic inventions of the twentieth century; it was an eccentric, syncopated mash-up of traditional measures and contemporary vernacular energy, an American motley with Elizabethan genes. Berryman uses the Dream Song form— three six-line stanzas, with lines of varying length and no predictable rhyme scheme—as a flexible variant on the sonnet. He needs this flexibility to accommodate the continually changing registers of voice, the sudden shifts of diction, and to allow him to keep so many balls in the air. He wrote a total of 385 Dream Songs over thirteen years, beginning in 1955. It was a period in which his mental and physical condition deteriorated as a result of extreme alcohol abuse, and the poems are nourished by that dissolution and the despair born of it, the best of them transmuting Berryman's condition into something lambent and ludic. Their protagonist, Henry, a shape-shifting tragicomic clown, is Berryman himself behind a set of Poundian masks. What makes the sequence such a signal achievement is that it manages to be at once representative of the poetry of its time and a radical departure from it.

For what then seemed a lengthy spell, from the late 1950s well into the 1970s, the standard-bearers of American poetry were a group of manic-depressive exhibitionists working largely, if not exclusively, in traditional meter and rhyme schemes, analysands all, and with self-inflating personae that always reminded me of those giant balloons of Mickey Mouse and Pluto associated with Macy's Thanksgiving Day parade. They published and reviewed one another in journals like *The Nation*, *The Partisan Review*, *The Kenyon Review*, and *The Sewanee Review*, with a good deal of autocanonizing. Robert Lowell, almost by default, it seemed, was ceded pride of place, the "most important American poet now at work." Lowell and Randall Jarrell, roommates at Kenyon College in the 1930s, and to a lesser extent Berryman, too, were big on rating and ranking: the top three poets, the top three oyster houses or second basemen, the three best Ibsen plays—they seemed especially to like the number three.

How do they rate now? It all looks a bit different fifty years on—it always does—after all the theatrics and hyperventilating, the crack-ups, ECT, Pulitzers, heart attacks, suicides, obituaries, followed hard on by biographies, critical appraisals and reappraisals, canonization and decanonization. This is the group sometimes known as "confessional" poets or "midcentury" poets: Lowell, Berryman, Jarrell, Delmore Schwartz, Sylvia Plath, Anne Sexton, Elizabeth Bishop, and Theodore Roethke. The last two were more peripheral, less overtly confessional, especially Bishop, and not so much on the scene, New

York or Ivy League (though Bishop turned up briefly, and memorably, at Harvard). Their work has stood up well: Bishop's stature is now generally acknowledged, Roethke's, unfairly, much less so. Jarrell, a fascinating and brilliant character, is remembered nowadays for his criticism and a novel about academic life, *Pictures from an Institution.* Schwartz became at twenty-five the first true star of that generation for his 1938 collection of poetry and stories, *In Dreams Begin Responsibilities.* He was adored by Berryman as a friend and revered by him for his poetry and intelligence from their early days as colleagues at Harvard; and by Saul Bellow, too, a close friend of both. Schwartz is read now, if at all, for his stories and best known for his protracted, wretched unraveling and decline, fictionally recounted by Bellow in *Humboldt's Gift.* Plath, a student of Lowell's, had the capacity for real linguistic artistry, but beyond the psychological violence and clamor—and her reign as one of the goddesses of victimhood, which brought her enormous attention—much of her poetry isn't worth revisiting. Sexton, also a student of Lowell's, is so calculatedly lurid and self-mutilating that the poetry very quickly bypasses mannerism and arrives at self-parody. "I was once known as the poet of madness, but now I am known as the poet of love," she said huskily of herself one evening at a literary event in Chicago. "You just wish they'd keep some of these things to themselves," Bishop, a manic depressive and alcoholic herself, told a *Time* magazine reporter in 1967. Indeed you did, and do. And Lowell? His prestige is much diminished (how could it not be?) and his influence—the stilted, hieratic tone and leaden gait of the early poetry; the self-mythologizing, the seamy show-and-tell of his breakdowns and private life—has been baneful. But there can be no mistaking his enormous gift, especially in phrasing and diction ("a savage servility / slides by on grease"), not to mention the matchless force and aptness of his descriptive language. Some of his poems are so indelibly part of the poetic voice of his era that, however much one might disapprove of him, to discount his importance is folly. His influence on Berryman and his poetry, directly and indirectly, was enormous, not least as Berryman began to catch up with Lowell in the mid-1950s and become a serious rival for what both perceived as the official culture's mantle of top poet, a position Lowell had held unchallenged since the publication of *Lord Weary's Castle* and his subsequent Pulitzer in 1947.

Hayden Carruth, born in 1921, who edited probably the finest—and certainly the most inclusive—anthology of modern American poetry in the last century, *The Voice That Is Great Within Us*, wrote in his introduction: "We had been born too late, that was our trouble. The great epoch of 'modern poetry' was in the past; its works, which we desperately admired, *The Waste Land, Lustra, Harmonium, Spring and All* and so many others, had been written long ago and had exhausted the poetic impulse. Nothing was left for us to do." The Chicago poet and editor Paul Carroll, born in 1926, wrote:

To a young poet the scene in American verse in the late 1940s and early 1950s seemed much like walking down 59th Street in New York for the first time. Elegant and sturdy hotels and apartment buildings stand in the enveloping dusk, mysterious in their power, sophistication, wealth and inaccessibility. One of the most magnificent buildings houses Eliot, his heirs and their sons; other tall, graceful buildings contain e.e. cummings, Marianne Moore, Ezra Pound, Wallace Stevens, and William Carlos Williams.

Eliot cast the longest shadow on the midcentury generation, not simply because of the brilliance of the poetry and essays: he was both the model and the antimodel for the New Criticism (espoused by Lowell and Jarrell's teachers John Crowe Ransom and Allen Tate). Eliot's work seemed to embody modernism for those who came after, and younger poets were trying desperately to find a way to get clear of him. Schwartz was the most obviously influenced by Eliot and would suffer both personally and as a poet through his inability to shake him off. In Berryman's case, early on at least, the voices of Yeats and Auden are most prominent, but he was certainly cowed by Eliot. In 1960, while writing his Dream Songs, he railed against Eliot's "intolerable and perverse theory of the impersonality of the artist." By then, for Berryman/Henry, it was very personal indeed.

Berryman's first successful poem in his mature style comes quite late, at the end of 1947, probably the most significant year of his life. He was thirty-three and his first book was about to come out. The poem is called "The Dispossessed." The first three of its ten stanzas read:

'and something that . . . that is theirs—no longer ours'
stammered to me the Italian page. A wood
seeded & towered suddenly. I understood.—

The Leading Man's especially, and the Juvenile Lead's,
and the Leading Lady's thigh that switches & warms,
and their grimaces, and their flying arms:

our arms, our story. Every seat was sold.
A crone met in a clearing sprouts a beard
and has a tirade. Not a word we heard.

Berryman seems to have known immediately that he'd made a breakthrough, rushing the poem into the book at the last moment and making it the title poem. The reader is not quite sure where the poem starts or where it's headed but quickly catches up, regardless. If you hear Gerard Manley Hopkins in there, you're hearing correctly, with the stressed syllables at the poem's beginning clustered together to suggest frenzy and urgency. The syntax is often described as "broken" or "crumpled." Dashes and ellipses indicate discontinuity of thought or sudden shifts in focus. The poem jumps here and there. Berryman, too, was jumpy, in body and mind. The movement is songlike, even dancelike, lyrical in an improvisational but coherent way.

Lowell is never lyrical. Of the very few contemporaries to whom Berryman paid serious attention, only Roethke has a similar ability to make his verse sing. The youthful Berryman was a splendid dancer—all the girls said so. That was before he began falling down with regularity and breaking bones.

"The Dispossessed" is one of three poems he wrote in December 1947. He had for some years been looking for an idiom for his jumpiness, a "nervous idiom." *The Dispossessed*, the volume, includes a series of nine poems under the title "Nervous Songs," each poem written in a separate voice, owing not a little to Rilke's *Die Stimmen* and Yeats's six-line stanzas. They are neither very good nor very nervous, but the scrambled diction and occasional use of dashes to indicate disjunction are already in evidence, along with the three six-line stanzas that would become the basis for the Dream Songs. Berryman was a nervous man: introverted, shy, skittish, easily rattled, neurasthenic, one who was described by others, and by himself, as "having no skin." He had been a bit of a hysteric and a drama queen from early in life, given to fainting dead away when in emotional distress or faced with conflict, even having psychosomatic epileptic seizures, as often as not to subdue his "difficult," possessive mother, who made him crazy but on whom he was helplessly dependent. He was also brilliant. Bellow, whom he would get to know at Princeton in the early 1950s, described him as "tallish, slender, nervous . . . [giving] many signs that he was inhibiting erratic impulses." That meeting with Bellow could not possibly

have been more significant for Berryman and his mature poetry. It was Bellow who would serve as the major catalyst in the
creation of the voice for the Dream Songs.

■

Berryman the poet was closing in on that voice, measure, form,
and idiom in 1947, even as Berryman the man was becoming
seriously unmoored. Married, happily, it would seem, for five
years to Eileen Mulligan (who, thirty-five years later, as Eileen
Simpson, by then a psychologist, would write *Poets in Their
Youth*, easily the most clear-eyed, intelligent, and compassion-
ate record of what it's like to live with and among poets), he had
begun an affair, the first since his marriage, with the wife of a
young colleague at Princeton. The affair generated a sequence
of 115 sonnets produced at white heat over the course of the
year.

There are quite a few gracefully rendered and successful
twentieth-century sonnets that cleave to the Italian, as in this
case, or Elizabethan model, and many more that play with or
deviate from that strict form in interesting ways (such as Ashbery's seventeen-line "And Others, Vaguer Presences"). Frost,
Larkin, Merrill, Heaney, and others succeeded in producing
modern sonnets in traditional form that feel natural in expression, as Yeats did with "Leda and the Swan"—still a dazzler. But
a long sonnet sequence along the lines of Sidney's *Astrophel and*

Stella isn't possible in the modern era. The conventions surrounding such an undertaking are no longer alive in the cultural consciousness. The form is too tidy, its strictures too inhibiting for so restless a century, in which even rhyme and meter seem to have become foreign to the general poetry reader's ear.

Hayden Carruth, reviewing Berryman's *Sonnets* in *Poetry* magazine, wrote that "the poems touch every outworn convention of the sonnet sequence." But he goes on to concede that "the stylistic root of the Dream Songs is present" in these sonnets in their "archaic spelling, fantastically complex diction, tortuous syntax, formalism, a witty and ironic attitude toward prosody in general." This is from sonnet 109:

> Ménage à trois, like Tristan's,—difficult! . .
> The convalescent Count; his mistress; fast
> The wiry wild arthritic young fantast
> In love with her, his genius occult,
> His weakness blazing, ugly, an insult
> A salutation; in his yacht they assed
> Up and down the whole coast six months . . last
> It couldn't: . . the pair to Paris. Chaos, result.

Though written in 1947, the sequence wasn't published until 1966. In an author's note at the beginning of the volume, Berryman writes: "These sonnets, which were written many years ago, have nothing to do, of course, with my long poem in process, *The Dream Songs*." Don't you believe it.

It was also in 1947 that Berryman began drinking heavily.

Curiously, given his later long-term and profound addiction, Berryman wasn't much of a drinker before the age of thirty-three (or much of a poet, for that matter). His wife, Eileen, had begun taking evening courses in psychology and wasn't around nearly as much to look after him. He needed looking after. The drinking escalated quickly into a large problem. He also began taking Dexedrine to get going in the morning and Nembutal to get to sleep at night. He was now traveling regularly to New York to see his psychiatrist, James Shea, in an attempt to stave off his depression. Whether Shea helped him is questionable; what is certain is that Berryman emerged newly fascinated with psychiatry and his own buried psychological issues, especially the suicide of his father just before his twelfth birthday, the story of which had been camouflaged by his mother. He also began to read the central texts of Freud, Fechner, Reich, and others, which made a tremendous impression on him. Freud and psychoanalysis were to become major themes for Berryman, as they already were for Schwartz and were about to be for Jarrell and Lowell. By 1953, Lowell was "gulping" Freud and telling one and all that he was a "slavish convert." These poets were, of course, not alone in their fascination. After the Second World War, with veterans returning en masse with psychological trauma, psychoanalysis—both the practice and the language associated with it—permeated the culture and country. Neuroses and mental illness acquired a sort of glamour, making their way into Hollywood, *Time* magazine, and the salon conversation of intellectuals. Schwartz, Lowell, Berryman, and

Jarrell probably didn't need the encouragement. Be that as it may, it was off to the races.

In the summer of 1948, Jarrell reviewed *The Dispossessed* in *The Nation*, sneering at "the slavishly Yeatsish grandiloquence in the early work, which at its best resulted in a sort of posed, planetary melodrama, and which at its worst resulted in monumental bathos." These poems, Jarrell wrote, were "statues talking like a book." Berryman wasn't pleased, but he wasn't surprised either: an entire generation of poets lived in terror of Jarrell's devilishly crafted turns of phrase. At least Jarrell also suggested promising developments ahead for *The Dispossessed*'s author.

Earlier in 1948, Berryman had begun a long poem about the seventeenth-century American poet Anne Bradstreet. He finished one stanza and then let it languish for five years. In its final form, *Homage to Mistress Bradstreet* runs to fifty-seven stanzas of, for the most part, eight lines each, the form modeled loosely on Yeats's aabbcddc stanzas (used in a number of poems including "A Prayer for My Daughter"). In Berryman's variant the syllable count ranges from three to twelve, with the rhyme scheme mostly abcbddba, though he does depart from this on occasion, as here:

> torture me, Father, lest not I be thine!
> Tribunal terrible & pure, my God,
> mercy for him and me.
> Faces half-fanged, Christ drives abroad,

and though the crop hopes, Jane is so slipshod
I cry. Evil dissolves, & love, like foam;
that love. Prattle of children powers me home,
my heart claps like the swan's
under a frenzy of *who* love me & who shine.

Homage to Mistress Bradstreet is much admired and little
read, its clotted syntax not permitting enough air to let the piece
breathe. One feels the strain in its assemblage. Berryman was
striving for a masterwork, something to rival Lowell's *Lord
Weary's Castle.* The sonnets, which also suffer from strangling
syntax, are livelier and more engaging, if mostly as clearer mark-
ers of where Berryman is headed in the Dream Songs.

Berryman regarded himself as a poet-scholar in the tradition
of A. E. Housman. He was foremost a Shakespeare scholar. He
had caught the bug while studying at Columbia in the 1930s
with Mark Van Doren, who took the rather troubled young man
under his wing and excited him about literature, Shakespeare
especially. When Lowell and his then wife, Jean Stafford, invited the Berrymans to their summer home in Maine in 1946,
everyone got on famously, and a visit meant to last a weekend
went on for two weeks. Berryman hadn't enjoyed talking to another poet so much since his days at Harvard with Schwartz.
Lowell remembered Berryman on that visit as "all ease and
light" as they sat by the mill pond talking about poetry, reciting
"Lycidas," comparing the virtues of Browning, Tennyson, Hopkins, Arnold, Swift, Dunbar, Henryson, Chatterton, Chaucer,

and Gray. Lowell noted the value of Berryman's hard work on Shakespeare, listening to him "quote with vibrance to all lengths, even prose, even late Shakespeare, to show what could be done with disrupted and mended syntax." Later on, Lowell would remember Berryman's fascination with syntax and recognize that it was "the start of his real style." Berryman thought of the visit as the "last summer of his innocence." Lowell's life was about to change, too: the breakup of his marriage to Stafford, the Pulitzer for *Lord Weary's Castle*, and the first in a series of manic-depressive breakdowns requiring hospitalization.

■

Berryman was at Princeton on and off between 1946 and 1953 thanks to various fellowships and low-level teaching jobs. It was an intellectually exciting place to be: R. P. Blackmur, Allen Tate, the European émigrés at the Institute for Advanced Study— Thomas Mann, Hermann Broch, Erich Kahler, Erwin Panofsky, the mathematicians Hermann Weyl and John von Neumann, the physicists Albert Einstein and Wolfgang Pauli—and there were frequent visits from distinguished speakers such as Eliot. Berryman, in spite of himself, was thoroughly charmed by Eliot. Other poets who made appearances included Yvor Winters, Lowell, Jarrell, Schwartz, and Roethke, who punched a psychiatrist at a cocktail party because he thought the doctor was there to take him away to a psychiatric facility. There were lots of parties. This was really the first generation of university poets, poets employed as scholars and lecturers instead of as physicians, farmers, bankers, or insurance surety lawyers.

At the beginning of 1953, Berryman took a walk around Lake Carnegie in Princeton with Monroe Engel and Saul Bellow, whom he'd met before several times but always in the presence of others. He quickly took to Bellow's sense of humor. A few days later he came home with a typescript of *The Adventures of Augie March* and took the weekend off to read it, finishing it in one big gulp at 4:00 on the Sunday morning. It had a dramatic effect on him. After reading it, he went back to his Bradstreet poem, which he had been stuck on since 1948; now he began roaring along, finishing it on March 15. Edmund Wilson called it "the most distinguished long poem by an American since *The Waste Land*." Lowell was hardly less enthusiastic.

When Bishop read *77 Dream Songs* in 1964, the year Lowell's *For the Union Dead* and Roethke's *The Far Field* came out, Berryman's poems confused her. "I'm pretty much at sea about that book," she wrote to Lowell. "Some pages I find wonderful, some baffle me completely. I am sure he is saying *something* important—perhaps sometimes too personally?" In a later letter to Anne Stevenson, after she had got her bearings, she wrote that Berryman echoed

"The Wreck of the Deutschland," Stevens, Cummings, Lowell, a bit, Pound, etc, etc.—but it is quite an extraordinary performance, although I think I really understand probably barely half of it. If I were a critic and had a good *brain* I think I'd like to write a study of "The School of Anguish"—Lowell (by far the best), Roethke, and Berryman and their descendents like Anne Sexton and Seidel, more and more anguish and less and less poetry. Surely never in all the ages has poetry been so personal and confessional—and I don't think it is what I like, really—though I certainly admire Lowell's.

Bishop is pretty sharp so far as the influences go. I don't see much of Stevens, though Berryman read and admired him a great deal ("better than us; less wide," he wrote in a eulogy for Stevens, "Dream Song 219"). Certainly Pound, whom Berryman not only admired but was in frequent touch with. I'd suggest there's a fair bit of Roethke in the mix, perhaps as much as or more than Lowell, and, among others, another Elizabethan, Thomas Nashe, whom Berryman regarded as "one of the masters of English prose," noting in particular among his techniques the "inversion or rearrangement for rhythm, emphasis, and simulation of the (improved) colloquial."

So what happened between 1948 and 1955 to turn an able scholar and mildly interesting poet into the author of one of the liveliest poem sequences in the modern era? This is late in any poet's career, though not unique: Stevens was thirty-five when his first serious poems appeared in *Poetry* magazine in 1914 and forty-four when *Harmonium* was published. Here is the swirl of circumstances: Berryman's behavior was getting more extreme by the week, his marriage was in tatters. He finished a highly psychologized critical biography of Stephen

Crane. He replaced Roethke for a term at the University of Washington in Seattle; lectured briefly at the University of Vermont; met Jarrell, without any fur flying. In 1952 he spent the spring term at the University of Cincinnati, a generally successful visit; he finished *Homage to Mistress Bradstreet*, which was published the following year in *Partisan Review*; he separated from Eileen and moved to New York City. In 1954 he taught creative writing at the Iowa Workshop, then summer school at Harvard; he returned to Iowa in the autumn and was forced to resign after a drunken incident. Allen Tate brought him to Minneapolis, where he began a long period of dream analysis and the following autumn started teaching at the University of Minnesota. On August 12, 1955, using 650 pages of dream analyses he had collected over the previous nine months, he began a poem in six-line irregularly rhyming stanzas that makes use of baby talk, blackface speech, religious allegory, and dreamlike slips of the tongue. On August 21, picnicking on the Apple River in Wisconsin with a few colleagues and their wives, Berryman conceived of a title for the new sequence: *Dream Songs*. He pressed a little piece of paper with a poem written on it into the hand of his colleague Ray West. "A small poem about a clown, as I recall," West said, "a poem about a jolly old man."

Berryman said that the model for *The Dream Songs* was Whitman's "Song of Myself," "the other greatest American poem," he told *The Paris Review*. ("It also has a hero, a personality, himself.") Berryman developed his narrative, he said, partly out of my gropings into and around Henry and his environment and associates, partly out of my readings in theology and that sort of thing, taking place during thirteen years—awful long time—and third, out of certain preconceived and partly developing as I went along, sometimes rigid and sometimes plastic, structural notions. That is why the book is divided into seven books, each book of which is rather well unified, as a matter of fact. Finally, I left the poem open to the circumstances of my personal life.

I would take the "structural notions" and "seven books, each book of which is rather well unified" with a barrel of salt. Berryman was certainly reading "Song of Myself," though I can't find any clear echoes of it in *The Dream Songs*. Let me suggest one or two other forces at play: the Dream Songs are all about voice, or voices. In them, for the first time, Berryman achieves a convincing speechlike voice. *Augie March* had principally revealed to him the possibilities of voice passing through a variety of registers—from smart street talk to highfalutin intellectual discourse—and the possibilities of humor, especially mixed with disappointment, suffering, or hardship. There's not a lot of that in Lowell, Jarrell, Plath, et al. Berryman would have been drawn to the immediacy and candor of Bellow's narrator, his almost autobiographical rendering of the quick succession of personal encounters and events in the novel. And he would have been exhilarated by the vitality of the writing. In 1963 he told Bellow that he would "be dreaming out an agrarian existence" were it not for "the adrenaline heaved me by your raving masterworks," *The Adventures of Augie March* and *Henderson the Rain King*, which he pored over in manuscript and at proof stages. The first collection of songs, *77 Dream Songs*, is dedicated to Bellow and to Berryman's third wife, Kate.

■

Though psychoanalysis didn't help Berryman's alcoholism or state of mind, it did serve to open him up to his inner self, and it was amid the rubble of that excavation that he found his alter ego: messy Henry, destructive Henry, hateful Henry, devious Henry, pathetic, sozzled, recidivist Henry, self-loathing Henry, song-and-dance Henry, peccant Henry, grab-ass Henry, stricken-with-guilt Henry, Henry the enduring ruin. This old trickster was the spectacularly dysfunctional and desperate character Berryman had been describing to psychiatrists and his fellow patients in group therapy for years, trying and failing to defuse and repair him. This is from "Dream Song 4":

'You are the hottest one for years of night
Henry's dazed eyes
have enjoyed, Brilliance.' I advanced upon
(despairing) my spumoni.—Sir Bones: is stuffed,
de world, wif feeding girls.

—Black hair, complexion Latin, jewelled eyes
downcast . . . The slob beside her feasts . . . What wonders is
she sitting on, over there?

The restaurant buzzes. She might as well be on Mars.
Where did it all go wrong? There ought to be a law against
Henry.
—Mr. Bones: there is.

"Henry does resemble me," Berryman told one interviewer,
"and I resemble Henry; but on the other hand I am not Henry.
You know, I pay income tax. Henry pays no income tax. And bats
come over and stall in my hair—and fuck them, I'm not Henry;
Henry doesn't have any bats."
    This is the first stanza of "Dream Song 28":

It was wet & white & swift and where I am
we don't know. It was dark and then
it isn't.
I wish the barker would come. There seems to be to eat
Nothing. I am unusually tired.
I'm alone too.

And this is the first stanza of "Dream Song 29":

There sat down, once, a thing on Henry's heart
só heavy, if he had a hundred years
& more, & weeping, sleepless, in all them time
Henry could not make good.
Starts again always in Henry's ears
the little cough somewhere, an odor, a chime.

In the introduction to the 1969 edition of his second collection of Dream Songs, *His Toy, His Dream, His Rest*, Berryman writes:

> The poem then, whatever its wide cast of characters, is essentially about an imaginary character (not the poet, not me) named Henry, a white American in early middle age sometimes in blackface, who has suffered an irreversible loss and talks about himself sometimes in the first person, sometimes in the third, sometimes even in the second; he has a friend, never named, who addresses him as Mr. Bones and variants thereof. Requiescat in pace.

Because of blackface Henry—who slips now and then into an old-fashioned minstrel show black speech—it's unlikely that *The Dream Songs* would find a publisher today, much less stand as one of the last century's most significant and admired poetic sequences. Berryman was interested in African American speech in the way he was interested in Thomas Nashe. It provided syntactic and verbal possibilities and a particular, subversive energy. Kevin Young, an African American poet who edited a *Selected Poems* of Berryman for the Library of America, had this to say on the subject:

> The fearlessness with which Berryman breaks through the polite diction of academic poetry into a liberating variety of idioms is a major part of his legacy. If Henry is a "monoglot of English / (American Version)," then Henry's blackface Mr.

Bones persona—a mask upon a mask—allows him to speak in dialect to reflect on his condition: "He stared at ruin. Ruin stared straight back. / He thought they was old friends."

The installment published in 1964 under the title *77 Dream Songs* contains nearly all the first-rate songs. There is a sharp falling off in *His Toy, His Dream, His Rest*, which contains a further 308 songs. The Henry mask begins to erode and with it the capacity for play and burlesque that manages to keep the poems buoyant instead of sinking into the self-indulgence typical of most of the "confessional" poetry from the era. The later Dream Songs are reduced to grim reportage from the front—often as not, a hospital bed in a ward for alcoholics. There is a lot of death; Berryman's friends die off one by one in the later poems. The effects of his long-term alcohol abuse became more evident and the hospitalizations increased. Schwartz's death, just after he completed *77 Dream Songs*, seemed to hit him hardest:

> This world is gradually becoming a place
> where I do not care to be any more. Can Delmore die? . . .
>
> I imagine you have heard the terrible news,
> that Delmore Schwartz is dead, miserably & alone,
> in New York: he sang me a song
> "I am the Brooklyn poet Delmore Schwartz
> Harms & the child I sing, two parents' torts"
> when he was young & gift-strong.

Henry is gone. No buffer. It's down to "I" now, the poet himself, alone. It is not one of Berryman's better songs and there's relatively little art to it, but its plainness renders grief more poignantly than the mirror and mask might have done. There would be more grieving ahead for Berryman. The title of Eileen Simpson's moving book about her marriage to Berryman, *Poets in Their Youth*, comes from Wordsworth:

> We poets in our youth begin in gladness;
> But thereof come in the end despondency and madness.

ROAD TRIP WITH THE MAESTRO

The Maestro is clearly moved by what he has just heard. I'd put us around Bobcat Flats between Fallon and Ely on US 50 in Nevada, which likes to call itself the "loneliest road in America." An article in *Life* magazine from 1986 quotes someone from the AAA saying of this 287-mile stretch: "It is totally empty. There are no points of interest. We don't recommend it. We warn all motorists not to drive there unless they're confident of their survival skills." It doesn't seem to me all that lonely, least not these days, but it's quiet enough. "I think I need to hold off a bit before we listen to the C Major," the Maestro says, at the end of Bach's D-Minor Partita for Solo Violin, recorded by Nathan Milstein in the mid-1950s. "And that's with one *l*," he growls. The Maestro likes to growl. He has a generally kind nature that can turn choleric at any moment for no apparent reason.

We're crossing a large swatch of land called the Great Basin. There are mountain ranges to either side, yellow sage along the roadsides, alkali wastes, military bombing ranges, ranch land, state parks. "Just when you thought he was bringing it to a close he manages to keep on going," the Maestro mutters to himself, shaking his head in wonderment. I ask him the next day what it was that affected him so deeply. "I wouldn't have the words to say," the Maestro offers reluctantly. "Maybe something about Bach and the landscape."

The Maestro plays the fiddle. I don't know how diligently he keeps up with it these days, but there's one on the crowded backseat of his '91 Camry along with a portable plug-in keyboard. He keeps his hand in by studying piano with Mr. Natural, or the individual on whom Robert Crumb's comic-strip character Mr. Natural is based. Mr. Natural teaches out of a storefront in the Haight in San Francisco, where the Maestro and I are longtime neighbors.

The Maestro regularly drives between San Francisco and Madison, Wisconsin, where he recently began keeping an apartment. He was raised in Madison. In fact, we were at college together at the University of Wisconsin forty-some years ago but, despite having friends in common, never met. I am the de facto replacement for the Maestro's usual companion on these trips, his rottweiler-and-something Tara, who, like the Maestro, was sweet-natured but unpredictable. "I wouldn't be trying to pet that animal," the Maestro would mutter darkly to dog enthusiasts who thought to approach Tara unbidden. Tara is gone now. That set the Maestro back for a good long while. I don't know that he's still not over it.

Fifty Septembers ago, John Steinbeck set out across America with his old standard poodle Charley as company. It was election season: Nixon-Kennedy. Steinbeck was fifty-eight, younger than the Maestro and myself, and near the end of his life. One can feel it in his writing. He was a smoker and drinker and on his third marriage. He'd had a couple of minor strokes. In two years he'd be awarded the Nobel Prize for Literature, and six years after that he'd be dead. It's long been fashionable for literary tastemakers to look down their noses at Steinbeck, and if you look for him in Louis Kronenberger's otherwise exemplary *Atlantic Brief Lives: A Biographical Companion to the Arts*, you'll be out of luck. Hard on the heels of Gertrude Stein comes Stendhal.

I read *Travels with Charley* only very recently, I suppose because I knew I would be making what would likely be my own last big road trip. I'm in the pink, don't get me wrong, but I'm not big on road trips and hadn't really made one in thirty-five years. This was an opportunity to see the rocks of Utah and Nevada that I'd been admiring from thirty thousand feet for more than half my life, and I had a two-week gig in St. Louis in late September I needed to make. I knew that, what with the Maestro and his new iPod, which he somehow beams into the car radio, we'd have a crackerjack listening experience along the way.

Bill Barich writes in his new book, *Long Way Home: On the Trail of Steinbeck's America*, that "at the core of *Travels* is a bleak vision of America's decline that [Steinbeck] chose to mitigate by telling jokes and anecdotes." Barich, who thinks less of *Charley* than I do, writes that Steinbeck told his editor Pascal Covici that the United States was suffering from "a sickness, a kind of wasting disease . . . Americans, overly invested in material toys and saddled with debt, were bored, anguished, discontented, and no longer capable of the heroism that had rescued them from the terrifying poverty of the Depression. And underneath it all," Steinbeck continued, "building energies like gasses in a corpse. When that explodes, I tremble to think what will be the result."

The Maestro was watching the speedometer and my hand on the stick, with its cruise-control button, like a hawk. We were driving south on US 93, the Mormon Trail, to Cathedral Gorge State Park, where we made a right turn onto 319, heading into Utah at the town of Panaca. In *The Nevada Desert*, Sessions S. Wheeler writes of the "great, jagged mountains of banded limestone rising high above desert valleys . . . To some it is austere and frightening; to others it has a lonely grandeur which is friendly and comforting." I was sort of digging the lonely grandeur when the Maestro called up some Troy "Trombone Shorty" Andrews on the iPod, New Orleans brass funk. I hesitated before remonstrating because the Maestro is, after all, the Maestro, and of unpredictable humor. "Do you suppose we might find something else to listen to?"

The Maestro turned up the volume. "No."

I regard myself as neither an especially able driver nor an inept one. (Few males will admit to the latter.) "Functional" is how I would describe my driving. I have been told I drive "like an old lady." An older woman told me this. I admit to an appalling sense of direction. (No other male will admit to this.) And I am given to reverie, as no doubt others in my line of work occasionally are. But although 93 is a straight road, the Maestro is in conductor mode, glowering with concern in my direction like Toscanini staring down a dodgy woodwind section.

Olivier Messiaen was commissioned by Alice Tully to write a piece inspired by the canyons of Cedar Breaks, Zion, and Bryce in southwestern Utah. The composer enjoyed a mild form of synesthesia, which allowed him to hear colors. The red and orange of the sandstone cliffs got him going, along with the "immense silence." A devout Catholic, Messiaen's tone poem *Des canyons aux étoiles* is meant to "glorify God in all his Creation." It's an unusually orchestrated and gorgeous piece in twelve parts; the last, "Zion Park et la cité céleste," is especially haunting. The locals were so excited that they renamed a mountain after him, near Cedar Breaks.

I don't really do eternity or quietude, and the open-air museum of forms we encountered that long day filled me with anything but that feeling. I might as well have been snorting coke for eight hours. I've never seen anything in my life so startling and visually commanding, bend after bend, mile after mile: earthworks, citadels, the funerary monuments of Petra and Aleppo, Afghan battlements, cliff fortresses, vast kilns. I imagined I saw before us rock-carved Hindu temples ca. A.D. 1000: the ornate towers of the Bhubaneswar temples; or, even more, the Sun Temples at Modhera in Gujarat and Konark; or, above all the rest, the temples of Khajuraho with their erotic friezes, the female figures, half turned toward the viewer, ever in movement, frozen in alluring gesture—nature imitating art imitat-

ing nature. All of it carved by the wind into the Navajo red sandstone.

So what sort of sound environment did the Maestro come up
with for this remarkable drive? Messiaen? More Bach? Ligeti's
glacially mutating sound clusters? Not quite. Best as I can recall, we started out with Merle Haggard as we climbed along 9
out of St. George toward Zion, past scattered groups of houses
that looked provisional and out of place in the inhuman landscape: from a distance like lichen and, on closer inspection, like
blight. Monk and Coltrane at Carnegie Hall, Nat King Cole (the
After Midnight Sessions with Sweets Edison, Stuff Smith, and
Juan Tizol), Ralph Stanley and his Clinch Mountain Boys, Ray
Charles. And toward the end of the day, with the setting sun doing something wonderful with the sandstone in the precincts of
Lake Powell, we had a medley that included Clarence Williams
("You're Bound to Look Like a Monkey When You Get Old"),
Van Morrison ("Caravan" and "The Healing Game"), and Va-
laida Snow, the remarkable hard-swinging woman jazz trum-
peter and vocalist, singing "Nagasaki" in July 1937:

> Hot ginger and dynamite,
> That's all they have each night,
> Back in Nagasaki where the fellows chew tobaccy,
> And the women wicky-wacky woo!

And Laura Nyro. "I know her. I forget her name. She's dead,
right?"

"You don't know shit," the Maestro snarled. He was rendering me a service that, nowadays, in the absence of my mother and father, a number of my close friends feel obliged to perform. They are reminding me, in case I had forgotten, that (1) I don't know shit, or (2) I'm full of shit, or (3) (when stronger medicine is required) I am shit. I'm grateful for this, but I don't know why it was necessary to wait another twenty miles before sharing Ms. Nyro's name with me.

The literature of car trips across America usually revolves around colorful local characters the narrator meets along the way. This is true of Steinbeck, Kerouac, William Least Heat-Moon in his *Blue Highways*, and so on. Even the insufferable Henry Miller, in his 1945 volume *The Air-Conditioned Nightmare*, has his unrelieved bombast interrupted by a mechanic in Albuquerque called Dutter. But the Maestro and I weren't doing interesting locals. I have no doubt they were there to be found in the hills, but we were following a plan, a loose plan to be sure, but a plan of sorts. This involved spending our evenings in Super 8 motels. The Maestro knew every Super 8 from the Pacific Ocean to the Mississippi that allowed dogs. Why we had to stay at dog-friendly motels when there was no longer any dog seemed to be beside the point. We would lunch at fast-food places along the way. This was not good. In the evenings we would dine where we could, usually a chain restaurant like Ruby Tuesday, where the task was to find something that came without "special sauce." The Maestro would have a shot of Jim Beam straight up. I'd have a double Maker's, rocks. We would return to the Super 8, check the map, and retire to our respective rooms. The Maestro would follow the fortunes of the San Francisco Giants on his computer. I would read about rocks until I could no longer read about rocks. Thus our evenings ended. Our days began early.

Our Utah adventure was meant to conclude at the aptly named town of Blanding, population three thousand and something, in southeastern Utah. On arriving there we learned that there was an all-terrain-vehicle convention and there were no motel rooms for at least 120 miles. The streets were empty, although there were, here and there, a few oversized motorized tricycles with big fat tires. It was mysterious, all right. It had already been a long day, and the Maestro had decided that it was less taxing for him to do the driving than to scowl at me for hours on end. The Maestro is an excellent driver and most at home behind the wheel. He made his living for forty years driving a taxi, an occupation from which he has now retired so that he can devote himself entirely to following the ponies, a subject on which he is expert.

There is nothing, or hardly anything, between Blanding and the Colorado town of Cortez but a great deal of particulate fecal matter in the air and some sort of bug, in plaguelike abundance, attacking the windshield. The road is dark. The road is long. The Maestro is not finding a clear radio channel to accommodate his iPod. To my alarm, in the dark of night on a narrow two-lane road, in the middle of truly-fucking-nowhere, the Maestro pulls over to the shoulder and puts his head in his hands. This is not good. He maintains that posture for some time. But then he rallies. He takes a deep breath and attacks the radio in earnest until he finds a quiet place. He turns on the car light. Ten billion shit-covered insects swarm the vehicle. He has found what he was looking for. It is Clifford Brown and Max Roach. It is 1954 in Los Angeles. With Harold Land on tenor sax and Bud's younger brother Richie Powell playing piano, George Morrow on bass, they are playing "Daahoud," and playing it as well as it can possibly be played. The Maestro takes a deep breath. "Like medicine," he says.

We drive up a mountain in the Colorado Rockies. We have lunch along the way in Telluride, as there are no McDonald's along this scenic stretch. The town is a horror, a yuppie hellhole, like Berkeley's Fourth Street Mall but at eighty-seven hundred feet. We drive up the mountain. We drive down the mountain. Phillip Walker, the New Orleans bluesman, is singing "I Got a Sweet Tooth":

> You're like a cake and ice cream
> You're a chicken 'n' rice
> You taste so good to me, woman
> Talkin' about each and every bite . . .
> I got a sweet tooth for you, baby
> I'm gonna lip-tease you . . .

We are driving across America, making time: the fields of amaranth, grain elevators, and silos of Kansas. Dead cows by the side of the road. Clouds shaped like cows. A hawk glides over the Boone Creek Baptist church. We're crossing the Ozarks, listening to Woody Guthrie:

> Hitler wrote to Lindy, said "Do your very worst."
> Lindy started an outfit that he called America First
> In Washington, Washington.

We pull into the Super 8 in Springfield, Missouri. We ask the woman behind the desk if there's a place downtown we can get a drink and a decent bite to eat. The fellow standing beside us, waiting for his receipt, says, "What downtown?" There are no more downtowns, haven't been for a thousand miles. The next night we stumble on a Victorian bed-and-breakfast in Cape Girardeau, placed between two gas stations on the edge of the black ghetto. Gay owners, ornate fixtures, very upholstered. We can't believe our luck. There is no Cape Girardeau, just chains out on the highway and a slum here on the banks of the Mississippi. And this unexpected oasis. They serve food. One of the partners, "the Chef," is very, very serious about his food. We have a couple of drinks. We make ready to dine. Two local middle-aged couples dressed in warm-weather-midweek-out-to-dine-Midwestern-pastel-cotton-sportif are seated before us. They are in good spirits, sharing news and comparing their days. The Maestro is outraged. "Why do I have to listen to these philistines talk the shit they talk?" he broadcasts at alarmingly inappropriate volume. The couples fall silent. I make a face.

"Ah, they can't hear me, I'm talking to you, not to them," and stalks off to get his iPod on which he plays first Diana Krall's recent disc *Quiet Nights*, one of my contributions to his iPod. It is lovely listening, no question. Then he plays Etta Jones's "Don't Go to Strangers." We're now killing off a bottle of red. "How come you're such a fuddy-duddy?" the Maestro barks. "These idiots behind us don't even know the owners here are homosexuals."

The Maestro wants to drive down to Memphis, to have a drink at the Peabody hotel. That's rather a long way to go for a drink, but the Maestro has sentimental memories of this particular hotel, something about the management letting ducks loose around the fountain. It is a very nice hotel, carved mahogany, coffered ceiling. The woman tending bar is Polish. This delights the Maestro, who tries out a bit of family Polish. There is no Memphis. Just the Peabody and Beale Street. And Beale Street isn't Beale Street anymore.

The Maestro wants to go to New Orleans. No time for that, I say. I had wanted to go and hang around Davenport or Rock Island, up the river, find an old hotel by the water, listen to Jack Teagarden play the trombone and sing "You Took Advantage of Me." I had wanted to read the poems of Dave Etter, a poet of the region dear to my heart. I had wanted to reread his book *Go Read the River.* Maybe the first book of poetry I ever bought, at the uptown New York Port Authority, 178th Street, in 1966. I had wanted to read the book, read the river, listen to Jack Teagarden, and drink some whiskey on a veranda at the end of September on the Mississippi. "Where have you been for the last forty years, Aug?" the Maestro says. By which he is implying that there is no old hotel down by the river where I can sit at dusk reading the river, reading Dave Etter, listening to Jack Teagarden, and drinking whiskey.

■

We are driving back from the Bonne Terre maximum security prison outside St. Louis listening to Charlie Feathers: not the Maestro and me—he's gone on to Madison—but my host Professor D.J. and me. That's Charlie Feathers, the Memphis musician. Sam Phillips at Sun Studio never knew quite what to do with Charlie; tried to steer him to the country end of things when he was more truly a rockabilly. Too bad for Charlie. Made for a difficult life, or more difficult than it should have been. He's a better listen than Elvis or Johnny Cash or the rest of the white boys who came out of Sun.

I was reading my poetry to the convicts at Bonne Terre. I'd say it was the most enjoyable reading I have ever given, even better than the one at the Harold Park in Sydney, a pub attached to a harness-racing track, twenty-three years ago, but everyone in the audience was drunk at that one. The prisoners seemed to like me just fine; not so much one of the social workers in attendance, who stood up at question time and said, "You know what I think, having listened very carefully to your reading? I think you have a lot of anger." I told her there was plenty to be angry about. The killers really got a kick out of that one. At one point, in answer to a question—one of those questions you always get about how you go about writing—I said that there were a lot of fragments of uncompleted poems orbiting around in my head at any given time, like space garbage around the earth. When Professor D.J. introduced me, he told the audience that I often "struck a sardonic tone" in my poetry. I would not gainsay the professor. At the end of the reading, some of the killers approached me, each more timidly than the one before, to shake my hand and to thank me for the reading. I was very touched; to be honest, as touched as I have ever been by an audience after a reading. One particularly large con, older than the others and more than a bit reticent, came up to me and leaned over: "You know what?"

"What's that?" I asked.

"I got a lot of that sardonic space garbage orbiting around in my head, too."

E. E. CUMMINGS

E. E. Cummings is the sort of poet one loves at the age of seventeen and finds unbearably mawkish and vacuous as an adult. But in the mid-twentieth century he was the most popular poet in the United States after Robert Frost, and from early in his career, among the most admired by writers and critics. It wasn't just the usual modernist suspects like Pound, Williams, Stevens, and Marianne Moore who sang his praises, but other, very different kinds of poet, too: Robert Graves, Dylan Thomas, Octavio Paz, Louis Zukofsky, and Charles Olson. As did any number of critics: Edmund Wilson, Harry Levin, Jacques Barzun, Lionel Trilling, Guy Davenport. Were all of them hornswoggled, taken in by the surface polish and acrobatics of Cummings's style and, those who knew him, by his great personal charm, unable to register the paucity of content, limited range, and shallowness of his work? The short answer is yes.

Cummings's innovative style was a perfect reflection of the modernist Weltanschauung: he dismantled, fractured, and reassembled traditional forms; cocked a snook at the canon and at received opinion; he was radical, not only in technique but also in his challenging of contemporary notions of propriety, status, decorum; above all else, he made it new. He arrived at his mature style early, by the age of twenty-three or so, in 1916, and his approach to form didn't alter or develop in any significant way. And perhaps it wasn't that new after all: there are examples of visual poems in English as early as the Elizabethan era, many of which he would have known. It's less clear how well he knew Mallarmé's *Un coup de dés jamais n'abolira le hasard* (1897), or the work of Apollinaire, who by 1916 had almost finished his *Calligrammes*, perhaps the closest thing to Cummings's poetry, if more pictorial in emphasis—the calligrams form images of a bunch of flowers and a bird, or the head and front legs of a horse.

As Guy Davenport pointed out in the 1980s in an essay terribly titled "Transcendental Satyr," Cummings's "eccentric margins, capricious word divisions, vagrant punctuation, *tmeses*, and promiscuously embracing parentheses" resemble the texts he read as a Greek major at Harvard. The first passage here is by Sappho; the second by Cummings:

[   ]
Her [
Man [
And see[ms
These girls al[l
Topmost [
Wanders [
[   ] these [
[   ]
Partner [
Own cousin [

Elbows [

Laughing away [

■

(Fields Elysian

the like,a)slEEping neck a breathing a   ,lies
(slo wlythe wom a pa)ris her
flesh:wakes
           in little streets

Many commentators have suggested that Cummings's use of the lowercase was intended as a populist move, an announcement that he, like Chaplin, was a little guy, an everyman. Davenport speculates more convincingly that Cummings got the notion from Don Marquis's comic newspaper column *Archy and Mehitabel*, which first appeared in 1916 and featured Archy, a former vers libre poet who had been reborn as a cockroach, and wrote poems and stories on an old typewriter. Since Archy couldn't use the shift key at the same time as the letters, his poems were, of necessity, in the lower case. The column was illustrated by George Herriman, creator of *Krazy Kat*, a comic strip that first came out in 1913 and that Cummings was mad about (he wrote the introduction to the first collection of the strip in book form in 1946). He loved the mad, Dada-inflected burlesque as well as the unique, phonetically spelled patois that incorporated any number of dialects and languages. Cummings himself was a tireless mimic, both on the page and in performance among friends. He could do low-life street talk or a delicious impersonation of T. S. Eliot.

Cummings always cited Ezra Pound as his main influence in terms of the visual organization of words and lines on the page, and the use of line lengths and spacing to follow the patterns of speech. The two first met in Paris shortly after the end of the First World War, and Cummings was immediately drawn to the older poet's "gymnastic personality," as he described it in a letter to his parents. Both men were possessed of an electric vitality. Both were attractive, brilliantly talented, puerile, and resolute in their ambition to revolutionize the medium of poetry. That first meeting began a lifelong friendship: Cummings, who shared Pound's anti-Semitism, was one of the few who kept in touch with him throughout the Second World War when he was broadcasting on behalf of Mussolini.

The key to Cummings is his exaltation of the condition of childhood. He was in thrall to the notion of the child's capacity for wonder, natural spontaneity, openness, playfulness. In much of his poetry he is seeking to tap the child's freshness in experiencing the world around him:

> i like kissing this and that of you,
> i like,slowly stroking the,shocking fuzz
> of your electric fur,and what-is-it comes
> over parting flesh. . . .And eyes big love-crumbs,
>
> and possibly i like the thrill
>
> of under me you quite so new

This is one of Cummings's better poems, and it was written early, as most of his memorable work was ("Buffalo Bill 's," "the Cambridge ladies," "in Just-"). The poem is adolescent in outlook—and oh, how I and countless other adolescents have been enchanted by it—but Cummings, both poet and man, never evolved beyond adolescence. The pronouns he favors here are "I" and "you"; this remained true throughout his work. It is one characteristic that distances his work from most modernist poetry, in which the use of the first person is uncommon, especially the breathless, faux-naïf first person. The diction is simple in the extreme, another characteristic of all his work. It also contains some of the words he liked to recycle. He would use the same ones in poem after poem: "young," "sudden," "keen," "delicious," "kiss," "thrilling," "sweet," "stars." The word "flowers" turns up nearly fifty times in his first collection, *Tulips & Chimneys*, published in 1923. Some of his sonnets— the above is one of scores—stick close to the traditional sonnet form, others take liberties with it; but the idiosyncratic typography makes them look more mold breaking than they are.

Occasionally, though, typography takes over and makes a poem work interestingly, kinetically:

> silence
>
> .is
>
> a
>
> looking
>
> bird . . .

Cummings here manipulates words and letters to achieve his effects, unsullied on this occasion by the use of the first person and the other mannerisms that took over early and hardened with time. One of his chief gifts is to atomize and reorganize letters, words, punctuation, and parts of speech, and in that way disrupt our habituated ways of reading for meaning. By forcing the eye to move in unexpected ways, he choreographs in these more visual poems something like a dance of attention.

Then there is his satire, which is more successful than the childish wonder poetry. Perhaps having a mean streak, as Cummings certainly did, helps. Here he takes a potshot at Auden and Spender:

> flotsam and jetsam
> are gentlemen poeds
> urseappeal netsam
> our spinsters and coeds)
>
> thoroughly bretish
> they scout the inhuman
> itarian fetish
> that man isn't wuman
>
> vive the millenni
> um three cheers for labor
> give all things to enni
> one bugger thy nabor

One of his favorite poems, and the one he seemed to enjoy reciting the most, was Wordsworth's "Intimations of Immortality":

> Thou little Child, yet glorious in the might
> Of heaven-born freedom on thy Being's height,
> Why with such earnest pains dost thou provoke
> The Years to bring the inevitable yoke

Cummings tried hard to avoid the yoke. He never had a job, claimed not to read the papers, and tried to steer clear of all mundane concerns, distractions, or responsibilities, the better to experience the world as if for the first time when he emerged each day from the mews on Patchin Place in Greenwich Village, where he lived for most of his adult life, sketchbook in hand, probably headed for Washington Square Park, having partaken of his morning pear, "eaten with a fork in the French style," with a spot of brandy or a pill to calm his nerves.

He read the Wordsworth poem when he delivered his *six nonlectures* at Harvard in 1952–1953—"nonlectures" because he didn't like "intellectuals," and so just chose to read out some of his favorite poems, prefaced by a few general statements. Near the beginning of his first lecture, he announced that "while a genuine lecturer must obey the rules of mental decency, and clothe his personal idiosyncrasies in collectively acceptable generalities, an authentic ignoramus remains quite indecently free to speak as he feels. This prospect cheers me, because I value freedom; and have never expected freedom to be anything less than indecent."

He had begun reading in public in order to supplement his meager income: now that his mother was dead, he no longer received the small stipend she'd given him. One evening in 1958 he turned up at the private girls' school that Susan Cheever attended in Dobbs Ferry, about an hour's drive up the Hudson from New York City. Her father, John Cheever, drove her to the school. "Joey!" (Cheever's nickname) Cummings shouted when he spotted the writer, whom he'd first met in the 1930s. Cheever remembered that first meeting: Cummings's "last book of poetry had been rejected by every estimable publisher, his wife was six months pregnant by her dentist and his Aunt Jane had purloined his income and had sent him, by way of compensation, a carton of Melba toast." Now he was at the height of his fame and a seasoned public performer.

The Cheevers drove Cummings back to Greenwich Village. He was in good form, "unabashed and very funny," with "an astonishingly mobile face and a flexible dancer's body. He wasn't just an inspired mimic; he seemed to become the people he was imitating." The threesome stopped for a burger in the Bronx, where Cheever pulled out a flask and spiked the coffee. Cummings had heads turning with his imitations, including of Susan's headmistress. In fact, that evening he persuaded Cheever to move his daughter to a less uptight school, for which—as she writes in her new life of Cummings—she was forever grateful.

A future biographer could hardly have had a more charming introduction to her subject.

For all of the bumps along the way, Cummings had something of a charmed life. His father was a Harvard professor and Unitarian minister, his mother came from a distinguished Boston family. William James introduced the pair and became one of Edward Estlin's godfathers. As well as the grand house at 104 Irving Street where he was born, Cummings's family had a summerhouse in New Hampshire, which he would enjoy until the end of his life. He died there in 1962 of a brain hemorrhage while cutting wood, a month before his sixty-eighth birthday.

At Harvard he roomed with John Dos Passos and could hardly have had a better time, acting as boho, bolshy, and radical as Harvard boys of that era were allowed to be, while at that same time calling attention to himself as an avant-garde poet. He volunteered as an ambulance driver in the First World War and wound up being imprisoned by the French for "seditious behavior" after he was caught sending letters home that were deemed "detrimental to the war effort." His father was well enough connected to appeal to Woodrow Wilson, who helped procure the boy's release after three unpleasant months. While he was in jail, he gathered material for *The Enormous Room*, a graphically detailed account of his time in the Dépôt de Triage, La Ferté-Macé. It is his best work: direct, with no fancy typography, its narrator—for once—a keenly observant adult, unembarrassed by his own large intelligence.

After the war he wound up in Greenwich Village, mixing with the likes of Williams, Hart Crane, Marianne Moore, Edna St. Vincent Millay, Allen Tate, and Djuna Barnes, who also lived on Patchin Place, as Theodore Dreiser once had and Marlon Brando later would. He had become well regarded as an experimental poet, but he hadn't yet become famous. Then, in 1931, he visited the USSR and was horrified by what he saw. His disenchantment with communism and frankness about it was not well received by his friends in the Village, a number of whom ostracized him. His politics would drift ever farther right. His account of his time in Russia, *Eimi*, published in 1933, is written in his more experimental, Cubist-influenced style, and is largely unreadable. Viz.:

> "pahnyeemeyeoo, tovarich"
> the atremble wrinkling stood:stares;now for the 1st time I realise(that mount has eyes,that long long ago these eyes marvellingly were unafraid)some—perhaps fragment of an aspect,of a shadow,of that unexplorable negative thrown by the infinite mystery of old age. And quietly "I" said behind all wrinkles exquisite Theness "think you are like us"
> Now it might have been Theness which begat Aness

He spent most of the rest of his life in the Village. His work became ever more attenuated and more predictable, while he became more celebrated for it.

Susan Cheever is particularly good on Cummings's relationships with his wives. For all his poetic interest in it, Cummings seems not to have been too keen on sex. His first wife, who had been married to his best friend, and with whom he had his only child, found him more interested in sighing and professing his love. His second, an enthusiastic and serial adulteress, continually ridiculed him for his sexual inadequacy. He married her because his analyst, Fritz Wittels, a student and biographer of Freud, and the author of *The Sex Habits of American Women*, told Cummings that getting married would "make a man of him." His third, common-law wife, Marion, an actress and successful model who towered over Cummings, also from time to time sought comfort in the arms of strangers (including A. J. Ayer, which did not please the anti-Semitic Cummings). Cheever's book is written in a style reminiscent of a *Vanity Fair* article, and she is clueless about poetry, but the book moves along briskly. Its principal virtue is its brevity. There are already a number of biographies of Cummings, including two very good ones—Richard Kennedy's *Dreams in the Mirror* (1980) and Christopher Sawyer-Lauçanno's *E. E. Cummings: A Biography* (2004)—but who wants to read six hundred pages about this most unpleasant of men?

Cheever struggles with Cummings's anti-Semitism, treating it as a sociological phenomenon endemic to the era and his social circle, like heavy smoking, drinking, and lack of exercise. But with Cummings it was a bit more than that. The following document from 1939 is quoted in Sawyer-Lauçanno's biography. Penciled at the top of the typed page Cummings writes: "how well I understand the hater of Jews!"

The Hebraic they—it permeates everything,like a gas or a smell. It has no pride—any more than a snake has legs. Above all:it is low—this heavy,hateful shut something crushes-by-strangling whatever isn't it ... makes any quick bright beautiful beginning impossible—stops inspiration just as the spirit's lungs are opening:for it cannot endure free,loving,gay;its own imprisoning pain perpetually must revenge itself on every soaring winged singful bird!

Here he is writing to Pound in October 1941, with Leningrad under siege and the transfer of Jews to the east beginning:

Dear Ezra—,

whole,round,and heartiest greetings from the princess & me to our favorite Ikey-Kikey,Wandering Jew,Quo Vadis,Oppressed Minority of one,Misunderstood Master,Mister Lonelyheart,and Man Without a Country

re whose latest queries

East Maxman has gone off on a c-nd-m in a pamphlet arguing everybody should support Wussia,for the nonce. "Time" (a loose)mag says Don Josh Bathos of London England told P.E.N. innulluxuls that for the nonce writers shouldn't be writing. Each collective choisi (pastparticiple,you recall,of choisir) without exception and—may I add—very naturally desires for the nonce nothing but Adolph's Absolute Annihilation,Coûte Que Coûte(SIC). A man who once became worshipped of one thousand million pibbul by not falling into the ocean while simultaneously peeping through a periscope and sucking drugstore sandwiches is excoriated for,for the nonce, freedom of speech.

Then there was this, from Cummings's 1950 collection,
Xaipe:

> a kike is the most dangerous
> machine as yet invented
> by even yankee ingénue
> ity(out of a jew a few
> dead dollars and some twisted laws)
> it comes both prigged and canted

The last line of the poem originally read: "it comes both pricked
and cunted." The editor, Theodore Weiss, a Jew, objected and
had Cummings change it. The book won the Harriet Monroe
Poetry Prize and a fellowship of five thousand dollars from the
Academy of American Poets. But this is not the author of *Homage to Sextus Propertius*, *The Waste Land*, or *Journey to the
End of the Night*. This is the poet celebrated for:

> . . . the little
> lame balloonman
>
> whistles   far   and wee
>
> and eddieandbill come
> running from marbles and
> piracies and it's
> spring
>
> when the world is puddle-wonderful

MEMORIES OF

CHRISTOPHER LOGUE

It would have been a gray September day in Melbourne twenty-five years ago, lunchtime, that I was sitting in a car outside the ABC's Broadcast House, listening to Christopher Logue being interviewed by Terry Lane, a former Church of Christ minister, who was laying into Logue with an unholy fury. The onslaught culminated in Lane declaiming, "Did you, or did you not, Mr. Logue, claim the Queen of England is the Antichrist?" There was a long pause, after which Logue remarked, "Well, I don't remember exactly, but it does sound like something I might have said."

When he came out, Logue greeted the driver and owner of the car, Michael Heyward, the rather dashing coeditor of the literary magazine *Scripsi*, and then, with great ceremony, and in an accent that I had never encountered in life or on-screen, an invention, surely—theatrical posh, you might call it—said, "August, it is a *great* pleasure to meet you. I'm so glad that it's you that's come and not John *Ash*bery."

Lunch was a revelation. Logue was a gifted performer at table when he chose to be, and he seemed happy to perform for two dazzled young admirers. I was already a keen fan of his

Homer translations. To my delight and confusion, not long after first looking into the Homer, I took a date to see Ken Russell's *The Devils* and there was Christopher Logue as Cardinal Richelieu. Jeepers. I'd never been in the presence of such a grand personality before, who'd seen and known and done so much, in the more exotic realms of "culture."

We deposited Logue at his hotel after lunch. Christopher, I quickly learned, needed his nap after lunch. Heyward, along with his coeditor, Peter Craven, had conspired to bring Ashbery and Logue over to Melbourne for the inaugural Writers Festival. Ashbery had to cancel at the last minute and I was asked to step in. The catcalls from the back of the room we read in that evening, along with two Australian writers, went something like: "August who? What the hell kind of name is that? Where's Ashbery? We want John Ashbery." They were all poets, these piss-artists and larrikins, and we became friends soon afterward, but immediately after my reading I sat down wretchedly next to Logue. He turned to me, looked me in the eye, and said slowly, with none of his theatrical baloney, "I enjoyed that, August. I enjoyed that very, very much."

Logue was unsparingly kind and generous to me over the years I knew him. Once when he came to the Bay Area, to visit a friend in Nevada City, we spent some time together in San Francisco. While he was out one evening I wrote a poem about him, which mentioned an attractive young woman he'd met at a Laundromat and suggested she was perhaps not the brightest bulb on the block. I realize now that writing a poem about

Christopher and then handing it to him was like tap-dancing through a minefield. But he seemed to rather like it. He objected to some phrasing near the beginning, but when he got to the characterization of the young woman, he became very stern. "You must change this bit, immediately. I am going to insist. The girl was not stupid, not one bit; in fact, she was very, very intelligent. I remember that most clearly. You must change that part." Which I did, but not the first quibble. He liked the poem fine, except that first little bit.

It probably would have killed Christopher, if his heart hadn't given out first, to hear himself described as "kind." He certainly could be "difficult." Years after Logue and I first met, Faber arranged a confab in London. I forget the occasion and I wasn't there. Some chucklehead had seated Logue next to Thom Gunn at dinner. Had I been asked, I could have warned them . . . I believe the argument was about professional actors reading poetry aloud, a notion Christopher favored and Gunn deplored (I side with Gunn on this one). Gunn shied away from conflict of any kind; Christopher lived for it. The two men, both good friends of mine, had a low opinion of each other's poetry (Gunn described Logue's Homer as "too easy"). I think it was Hugo Williams that Thom said he turned to and pleaded, "Get me away from this man!"

At that first Melbourne Writers Festival, Logue and the actor John Stanton put together a dramatic presentation from portions of *War Music*. I've never witnessed a live performance of any kind that so thrilled me. The heat of it never relented, not for a moment, though it lasted well over an hour. The violence of the material seemed to course through the actors, Christopher especially.

I know, almost exactly, when Christopher began struggling with his memory. I received a phone call from him a day or two before we were to read together at the London Review Bookshop in November 2004. I hurried down to Camberwell Grove and we went off for lunch together at a local Mediterranean restaurant. I did my best to calm him about the loss of his faculties, but what was going on with him was real, and about to get worse. Regardless, Christopher agreed to give it a go, and we had one final reading together. He was a bit tentative that evening, compared to his usual confidence and force, but he was fine. I doubt anyone in the audience heard or spotted anything off about his performance. At dinner that evening, someone mentioned "children," and Christopher was off to the races. He "disapproved" of children, boy children in particular. They grew into murderous young adults, soldiers, slaughtering innocents, and so on. The girl children grew up to breed boy children, so they were to be disapproved of as well. A young mother, with small children, was very annoyed, if not outraged. Christopher enjoyed outraging people.

He would have had a rough go of it through the earlier part of his life. His rambunctious and contrarian temperament wouldn't have helped. But the twenty years or so from the time I first met him were the happiest of his life. He had met and married Rosemary Hill and, shortly thereafter, moved into the

house in Camberwell Grove. He had turned into a happy, pro-
ductive, relatively stable householder and distinguished man of
letters. It suited him.

I don't remember the occasion, or what may have prompted
it. It was not all that long ago. I'm certain it was in London,
probably a pub or restaurant. I said to Christopher, "You're
lucky, aren't you." The remark seemed to come out of nowhere
and caught him off guard. He paused a few moments, thinking,
then turned to me with a rueful laugh, looking me straight in
the eye, as he had done that first evening in Melbourne years
before, and said, "*Lucky?* You must be *joking.*"

A PEACOCK CALLED MIRABELL

James Merrill

James Merrill has in Langdon Hammer the biographer he would have wished for: intelligent, appreciative, sympathetic, thorough, a first-rate reader of the poems, and an excellent writer to boot. Merrill would have hated to be the subject of a lumbering, ill-written biography: he was all about stylishness and elegance, in poetry and in life. But *James Merrill: Life and Art* shows that you should be careful what you wish for. At 809 pages, not including a hundred pages of notes and index, this biography is about the size of *The Brothers Karamazov*, recounting in exhaustive detail the not especially eventful or interesting life of this least Dostoyevskian of writers. Poets' lives are seldom eventful or interesting. There's a great deal of looking out the window, pacing around, reading, writing, drinking, gossiping, complaining, especially about money and neglect, and more often than not ill-advised romantic attachments. Though money, or the want of it, was not among Merrill's complaints.

Merrill seems to have believed that his life was an extension of his poetry, both of them works of art. His own life, or his life recalled, was his principal theme, and Proust, with whom he fell in love during his first year at college, his principal model. The considerable archive he donated to the Olin Library at Washington University in St. Louis includes not only drafts of poems and letters but also notebooks, calendars, and guest books, along with more than fifty years' worth of diaries and journals, most of which no one but Merrill had ever read. He encouraged and in some cases paid friends and lovers, of whom there were legions, to donate letters they'd received from him to the Olin archive. Hammer mines this trove with tireless ardor.

Merrill's 2001 *Collected Poems* is much the same length as the biography, at 885 pages. A companion volume, *The Changing Light at Sandover*, which comprises three books and a thirty-seven-page coda, incorporates "supernatural communication" with assorted spirits including various deceased friends, Auden, Plato, and a peacock called Mirabell, all of it recorded with the help of Merrill's longtime partner, David Jackson, during twenty years of séances using a Ouija board at their home in Stonington, Connecticut. This volume tips in at 560 pages. Merrill also wrote plays, a memoir, and two novels. Born to enormous wealth, he had little to distract him from his writing apart from endless rounds of socializing and travel. His father was Charles "Good-time Charlie" Merrill, cofounder of Merrill Lynch, who earned his moniker through prodigious accumulation of money and women.

James Merrill was at the forefront of American poetry in the 1970s but is seldom read today. Despite this, he is a significant poet, preternaturally gifted, a master of form (meter and rhyme) and design, and often elicited comparisons with Mozart, who liked to boast that he "pissed" music. Busoni would be a better comparison with Merrill's huge technical skill, high surface finish, and complexity of design, much of it gratuitously decorative, and often with not terribly much going on underneath. Both had a large gift that was also a vice, one Merrill was certainly aware of, occasionally warred against, but usually succumbed to. Hammer, whose appreciation of his subject tends to lapse into worship, does not shy away from Merrill's virtuosity and the poet's own quarrel with it. Hammer met Merrill when, as a student at Yale, he was designated to pick up Merrill from Stonington and drive him to a reading. He was thoroughly charmed by the man whose life he now, as head of the English Department at Yale, exhaustively records. Hammer finds Merrill to be a wonderful, even exemplary man. It's hard to disagree: he was brilliant; his capacity for friendship and love, sexual and otherwise, appears to have been boundless; he was supremely generous to friends, and through the Ingram Merrill Foundation he established in the 1950s, to artists and arts organizations.

I never met him. I missed him by a semester when he was teaching at the University of Wisconsin in the spring of 1967. By all accounts, even his own, he wasn't much of a teacher but was a delightful presence. One of his students that term, Stephen Yenser, became not only a lifelong friend but also one of Merrill's very best readers, and coeditor, with J. D. McClatchy, of an excellent though overlong 2008 *Selected Poems*. Reading Merrill at length can feel like being trapped in endless rooms full of

Ming Dynasty black lacquer furniture with mother-of-pearl inlays, and flowering begonias painted on, along with birds and butterflies alighting on pomegranate stems—it's exquisitely fashioned but makes you want to find the sanctuary of a Shaker meeting hall where one might sit on a hard wooden bench and stare at not very much at all.

It didn't come out of nowhere. In one of his most restrained, and most successful, poems, from the sonnet sequence "The Broken Home," he provides this portrait of his father late in life:

> My father, who had flown in World War I,
> Might have continued to invest his life
> In cloud banks well above Wall Street and wife.
> But the race was run below, and the point was to win.
>
> Too late now, I make out in his blue gaze
> (Through the smoked glass of being thirty-six)
> The soul eclipsed by twin black pupils, sex
> And business; time was money in those days.

"I am a mixture of Santa Claus, Lady Bountiful, the Good Samaritan, Baron Richtofen, J. P. Morgan, Casanova. I am tender as a woman, brave as a lion, and can fight like a cat." This is the way Charles E. Merrill described himself. In truth, his considerable generosity notwithstanding, he was a rapacious monster. Merrill père can probably be credited with the introduction of the chain store—he developed the Safeway supermarket chain and was the underwriter for McCrory's five-and-dime stores as well as the Kresge chain, the "ancestor of

Kmart"—and regarded himself as a great benefactor of the common man. When he wasn't working, he was chasing women, who seem to have been pleased to be caught by the diminutive tycoon. "He was the banker as Jazz Age celebrity," Hammer writes, "in plus fours or a double-breasted Van Sickle suit, a confessed hedonist and the hardest worker going." James, his only child by his second marriage, to Hellen Ingram, seldom saw his father. His parents separated when he was eleven and divorced when he was thirteen; the breakup traumatized him.

When he was six, he wrote "Looking at Mummy":

> One day when she was sleeping
> I don't know who
> But it was a pretty lady
> That knows me and you.
>
> So, one day when she was sleeping
> I took "Mike" a-peeping
> The "do-not-disturb" was on the door.
> And I looked around the room and floor
>
> Then I looked to the bed
> Where that pretty head lay
> And the hair was more beautiful
> Than I can say.

It's possible that Merrill had some help with this composition from the subject of the verse, who "played rhyming games with her son when he was small" and "wrote doggerel" to please family and friends. Mike was the family's red setter. Merrill's mother was quite as formidable as her husband. Like him, she grew up in Jacksonville, Florida. After graduation she became a journalist, the society editor of Jacksonville's evening newspaper. Soon, she was putting out her own weekly social chronicle; she "sold ads, wrote the copy, corrected proof, pasted up the 'dummy,' rolled the magazines for mailing, and carted them to the P.O. to send them on their way." Miami was becoming a big tourist destination, and as Florida grew so did her paper, the *Silhouette*. During the summers, when society events slowed down, she went to New York to study journalism and fiction writing at Columbia. She befriended one of her teachers, Condé Nast, publisher of *Vanity Fair* and *Vogue*, and was soon attending his Manhattan parties.

In 1924, having heard that Charlie Merrill had separated from his first wife, Hellen wangled an interview with him. Charlie was fascinated. She was a professional, business savvy, and cultured, and she smoked and drove a car; she was not only a very lovely young woman but also a modern one. It was a love match, and it made perfect sense. Charlie sealed the deal when he had an "orange tree, heavy with fruit" delivered to Hellen's aunt, who had come to visit. As Hellen later put it, "No Southern woman could resist an orange tree in New York." James Merrill's half sister Doris would remember Hellen as a woman perpetually at her desk writing thank-you notes and invitations. Hellen and Charlie sought out New York society and, as with most else, conquered it. Throughout his life, Merrill would be intimidated by, if admiring of, his mother and her pluck. From "The Broken Home," written thirty-two years after "Looking at Mummy":

> Under a sheet, clad in taboos
> Lay whom we sought, her hair undone, outspread,
>
> And of a blackness found, if ever now, in old
> Engravings where the acid bit.
> I must have needed to touch it
> Or the whiteness—was she dead?
> Her eyes flew open, startled strange and cold.
> The dog slumped to the floor. She reached for me. I fled.

The "broken home" was 18 West 11th Street, a particularly lovely block of brownstones. The address became famous when the house was accidentally blown up in March 1970 by the Weather Underground. Merrill wrote a poem about the incident:

> In what at least
> Seemed anger the Aquarians in the basement
> Had been perfecting a device
>
> For making sense to us
> If only briefly and on pain
> Of incommunication ever after.

Charles Merrill's grandest and most favored residence was the Orchard, a thirty-acre estate in Southampton on Long Island, which he bought for $350,000 in 1926. Stanford White, a friend of the original owner, another Wall Street baron, designed the interior and ornamental bits in the garden. White was later shot by a jealous husband, a grace note that especially delighted Charlie. As a child, Merrill spent summers here with his half brother and sister from his father's first marriage. "This was the formative setting of Merrill's childhood," Hammer writes. "It showed him that a house could be a self-enclosed world, expressive of its owner. It left him both attracted to and resistant to everything that was grand."

While Merrill's adulthood was filled with privilege, fun, friendship, sex, and poetry, his childhood appears to have been unhappy. A sickly child with poor eyesight, whose thick glasses affronted his mother, he was coddled by servants but largely neglected by his parents and shunted from school to school as Charlie moved restlessly among his houses in New York, Palm Beach, North Carolina, Southampton, and Tucson. In 1933, when Merrill was seven, his parents hired as his governess a woman named Lilla Howard, whom Jimmy came to love. She seemed to have exotic European origins and, though not French, was to be addressed as "Mademoiselle." Merrill called her Zelly. She "gave him his first book of foreign postage stamps, and fussed over his ever-expanding collection with its scent of faraway places . . . She copied prayers and poems for him to read and memorize. She stitched costumes for his marionettes." He was a devoted puppeteer and would remain so, literally and figuratively, throughout his life. Merrill's older half brother, Charles, who rather resented his pampered relation, remembered Zelly as "a mix of intellectual seriousness and kindness, which Jimmy wasn't getting from Hellen."

■

When he turned thirteen, his parents now divorced, Merrill was sent off to board at the Lawrenceville School in New Jersey. He was a pudgy boy, hopeless at sports, bespectacled, brilliant in class, aloof, and distinctly effeminate. He of course immediately became the favorite subject of the kinds of torture boys inflict on one another in these environments. A favorite sport was being "depantsed," which involved the boys stripping Jimmy "naked, then rubbing his penis and anus with stinging peppermint oil" and then forcibly masturbating him. The boys "whistled when Jimmy crossed the campus with the swishy, hips-first walk the boy was developing." But Jimmy, finally, was Charlie Merrill's boy, and found a way to put a stop to his persecution. When cornered one day by a posse of louts, instead of being forcibly depantsed, he took his own trousers off in the teasing manner of a striptease. That put paid to the business. Merrill would later write that this was his first experience of "hate."

Lawrenceville in the early 1940s was no different from other boys' boarding schools in its rituals of hazing. What was different was the caliber of the education. Merrill made his first friend, a Jewish boy called Tony who wore pink and mauve cashmere sweaters and had "an imitation upper-crust drawl *and* a lisp." He tried his hand at writing poetry. He made more friends. He threw himself into theatrical productions, always plumping for the female roles, anything to put on a frock. From being an object of ridicule and abuse, he became an exotic character. His father was interested, from afar, in Jimmy's development as a poet, and remained so. In 1942 he paid for the publication of a small collection of poems and stories titled *Jim's Book*, which included a poem called "Mozart":

> Music free from passion, passionately played,
> Plumed with cool perfection, powdered with despair!
> Each delicious flourish daintily debonair,
> Purity on paper, brilliance on brocade!

Already, at sixteen, he was engaging with the dilemma he would struggle with for the rest of his writing life. As Hammer puts it, his work puts "artfulness and emotion at odds with each other; the strong feelings they involve—grief, moral outrage—are put out of reach by the conspicuous skill that evokes them."

He enrolled at Amherst College, as his father wanted. Charlie was an Amherst alumnus and a major benefactor. Jimmy usually went along, best as he could, with the wishes of his father, a distant but not malign presence in his life, in contrast to his overbearing mother. His half brother Charlie had insisted on going to Harvard, which enraged the old man. Merrill enlisted in the army in 1944. His bad eyesight kept him in the typing pool in New Jersey, almost certainly no hardship to the Allied cause. He was mostly bored, read and reread Proust, and mooned over one of his bunkmates. All that came of that was the bunkmate receiving an inscribed copy of Rilke's poems around the time Merrill was discharged, abruptly, in January 1945 (almost certainly as the result of string pulling by his father).

Over lunch in Amherst in September 1945, Merrill met Kimon Friar, the most influential person in his young adult life. Merrill was to spend a great deal of time, not least in his novels and memoir, exorcising his influence. Friar was a visiting instructor at the college and director of the Poetry Center at the 92nd Street YMHA in New York. Born on an island in the Sea of Marmara to Greek parents who immigrated to Chicago, he was, at thirty-three, fourteen years older than Jimmy: "short, wiry, and dark . . . a high-minded, charismatic man of letters and an unabashed self-promoter." (Hammer, to his credit, is protective of his subject and seldom refrains from discreetly revealing disapproval.) Merrill asked Friar to have a look at some of his poems. Friar groaned, but when he finally agreed to look, he was flabbergasted:

> I was thunderstruck . . . I called in Merrill and said: "You're already a superb poet. I cannot, of course, make anyone a poet who isn't one initially; I can only teach you all the techniques I know during the remaining time I have here . . . You must be willing, in this short period of eight months or so, to give yourself over to my dictatorial direction . . . I shall set you exercises in all forms of poetic techniques and, at the same

time, commission you to write for me about three poems a week embodying the lessons. I'll set the themes, the stanza forms, the meters, the rhyme schemes, and orchestration, everything . . . What do you say?"

"Try me!" Merrill replied.

Soon afterward the two became lovers; it was Merrill's first real homosexual affair. "I have been taught to love," he wrote operatically in his diary.

His mother found out what was going on, after opening a letter Merrill had sent Friar, and called Charlie, who convened a family war council. The notion was floated of hiring a mobster to have Friar "rubbed out." A "more seemly" suggestion, as Hammer puts it, was to engage the services of a "woman of loose reputation in Southampton, with an interest in the arts, who might be paid to introduce Jimmy to the pleasures of female flesh, then disappear." All that came of it was a call to Friar from Hellen telling him to cut it out, now.

Needless to say, that served only to inflame the romance. Merrill was enchanted by Friar's being Greek and by the ancient Greek notion of *erastes*, "the mentor and lover who helps the *eromenos*, a beautiful youth, to discover the passion for knowledge through their erotic relationship." Friar introduced Merrill to Cavafy's love poems. Merrill had studied ancient Greek; now he was learning the demotic. Finally, Hellen's disapproval was too much for Merrill, and he bailed on his lover. He couldn't "cope," he said, so he found a new "friend" for a while, and then another . . . He moved to New York and started on a lifelong round of dinner parties and soirées. He turned twenty-one, and the enormous trust fund that Charlie had set up for him and the rest of his children kicked in. He was suddenly a very wealthy young man.

This was a mixed blessing. He would always wonder, as the rich I suppose do, who his real friends and lovers were and who was in it for the free ride. But the money did allow him to live the sort of life he would have chosen for himself, and it wasn't an especially grand one. In 1956 he bought an ordinary enough three-story house in Stonington. He also traveled, of course, and bought a house in Athens, and in the late 1970s a place in Key West, but he was keener on giving money away than spending it on himself. He lived to read, write, travel, go to parties, pick up young men, fall in love with this one and that.

He visited Greece for the first time in 1950. Hammer's description of Merrill's first impressions of "Athens in its legendary 'purple dusk'"—and the excitement of the visit as a whole—may well be the best part of the biography: "Merrill was released then into the sensory revelation that was Greece. For the first time, he heard nightingales sing and peacocks cry. He strolled in Athens's 'extraordinarily lovely' gardens: 'Lemon and bitter orange flowering, the air filled with their odors—a sense of wafting that I have never before known.'" Friar, with whom Merrill had kept in touch, was his guide; but there was a growing unease between them, but the trip itself deeply affected him. Something about Greece, and not merely the very avail-

able young men, refreshed and exhilarated him, and he produced much of his best work there.

Merrill met David Jackson after a performance at the Artists'
Theatre in Greenwich Village of a play of Merrill's called *The
Bait*. During a soliloquy "heads swiveled as 'Arthur Miller and
Dylan Thomas . . . stumbled out,'" "passing judgment," as Hammer puts it, "with their feet." "I learned what Mr. Miller, with
uncanny insight, had whispered in Dylan's ear shortly after the
curtain rose," Merrill wrote years later in his memoir *A Different Person*, "You know, this guy's got a secret, and he's gonna
keep it."

Jackson's voice was the first thing Merrill noticed. He was
from somewhere else, somewhere in the American West. Lead,
South Dakota, was in every sense about as far as could be from
West 10th Street, where Merrill had moved on his return from
his trip to Greece. David was fair-haired, strongly built, heterosexual in manner, and sported a wedding ring. He was the son
of native South Dakotans, his father a failed businessman who
moved his family to Southern California in the 1930s, like so
many others from that part of the country. David grew up in a
down-at-heel part of L.A. until after the war when the family
moved to a new ranch house in Tarzana in the San Fernando
Valley. This was where, in 1954, David took Jimmy to introduce
him to his parents: George, "an irascible husband and father
who grew meaner, even brutish in old age," and Mary, a "for-
bearing" mother who was "funny, sweet, sociable, and a heavy

drinker." She also liked to tell stories and embellish, a trait her son seems to have inherited. (Among David's fibs were that he'd won the Purple Heart, that his uncle owned the magazine *Popular Mechanics*, and that his father had founded an airline.)

Jimmy and David rented a Volkswagen Beetle for the trip out west. In one of the most amusing scenes of the book—exactly the sort of scene a less comprehensive biographer would omit—the couple arrived in Tarzana. Jimmy offered to make dinner for the family, who would have much preferred dining out: he banished David's mother from the kitchen, "stood at the stove and produced the meal while wearing lavender knee socks and shorts and a lavender striped shirt. Then, at the table, he gobbled and sucked." David's wife, Sewelly, had also turned up for the gathering. (David and Sewelly had met and married in a heat at college and quickly discovered they were both gay but remained great friends.) Sewelly remembered that "Jimmy made so much noise—no one had taught him how to eat!" Later that evening Jimmy, David, and Sewelly, whom Jimmy immediately adored, went off to Laguna Beach, checking into a "superdelux" motel. They found a bar, where they proceeded to get tight. They drank some more back at the motel and "fell into one bed." The next day, Merrill wrote, the three of them "greeted the morning with all our old vigour, reading the funny papers on the little cliff where they served breakfast." "The photos from that Sunday breakfast," Hammer adds, "shine with mischief. With the Pacific crashing behind them, the sun beating down, and the comics spread out on the table, they made a lively, unlikely trio: two brand-new friends, two male lovers, and a devoted husband and wife." Sewelly would remain one of Jimmy's favorite people.

■

Episodes like this are the payoff of biographical exhaustiveness. Now for the costs. We learn that Merrill "had developed a painful hemorrhoid, which resisted Miss MacHattie's remedies. So Jimmy consulted the physician attending his father in Rome, Dr. Albert Simeons. A British-born endocrinologist with high-society clients, Simeons was, Jimmy found, 'a very charming man.'" Simeons recommended surgery and Merrill consented, though he was nervous. "He'd been reading the *Purgatorio*, and he viewed the operation as a spiritual trial—which it would turn into before he left the hospital. As they chatted prior to surgery, Simeons soothed his young patient, playing Virgil to this impressionable Dante, by dispensing consoling wisdom."

At least half of this biography wastes the reader's time with this sort of kapok. This raises a larger question: What is the function or purpose of such a detailed biography of a poet? Does it bring us closer or tell us more of what we would like to know about the work? I think not. Three or four top-flight essays, and they're certainly out there, perform that service far better. Late in life Merrill, who simply pretended that modernism never happened, read Hugh Kenner's *The Pound Era* with great interest. Merrill had no prior interest in Pound and the "heave" that broke the back of the pentameter. His view was: Why bother? The pentameter was just fine. But *The Pound Era* (at only 561 pages) is an intellectual biography, not only of the man but also of the milieu he worked and developed in, and at no point discusses issues to do with the poet's digestive tract. Kenner succeeded in bringing Merrill to read Pound seriously for the first time. I find it unlikely that Hammer, who makes very bold claims indeed about Merrill as a major figure in modern English-language poetry, will succeed in altering the opinion of the Merrill skeptic over the course of his heroically thorough undertaking.

Merrill continued to write and travel and entertain for the rest of his life, garnering prize after prize along the way. Did he deserve all the praise and prizes? Probably not, but more than most who win these awards. With its complex surfaces, formal dexterity, and irony, his poetry fitted the aesthetic priorities of the New Criticism, the prevailing literary theory of the time. All his collections contain superb individual poems, but for my money his best poetry is buried in his first Ouija board collection, *The Book of Ephraim*, but can be found only if one is prepared to wade through all the inane, CAPITALIZED utterances of friends and luminaries from "the other side." His voice is more intimate in these poems:

> My downfall was "word-painting." Exquisite
> Peek-a-boo plumage, limbs aflush from sheer

Bombast unfurling through the troposphere
Whose earthward denizens' implosion startles
Silly quite a little crowd of mortals
—My readers, I presumed from where I sat
In the angelic secretariat.
The more I struggled to be plain, the more
Mannerism hobbled me. What for?

Thom Gunn, in an enormously admiring essay, remarks of
Merrill's earlier work, "His poetry has been, typically, personal
and anecdotal, but the narrator was most comfortable as an almost anonymous observer . . . least comfortable at the center of
the poem, where . . . the treatment becomes positively rhetori-
cal. The rhetoric amounts to a kind of withholding, but I am not
sure of what." The verse of the Ouija board poems is freer; the
use of the board seems to have helped liberate Merrill from himself. He was an extremely controlled poet and human being. He
struggled to be less so. Greece also served him in this fashion.

James Merrill died in February 1995 of an AIDS-related illness. He concealed his illness from all but his closest friends and
handled his situation with as much dignity and consideration to
others as he was able to summon, even if he felt "beleaguered
by the number of old friends from far places" who visited him
toward the end. That was who he was. The poet Frank Bidart,
one of his older friends, is quoted near the end of Hammer's
book: "He was infinitely accomplished, preternaturally gifted—
the greatest rhymer since Pope—capable of doing anything on

the page, with a divine assemblage of sound and movement."
Money, Bidart goes on, gave Merrill the power to get "not
everything he wanted in life, but a lot [of it] . . . and Jimmy was
very aware of how lucky he was. Now all of a sudden he wasn't,
in a big way."

KENNETH COX

I first heard the name of Kenneth Cox, in the manner I first heard of many names that would become important to me, from Basil Bunting in 1971 when he was visiting at the University of Victoria in British Columbia. Bunting, who liked to say that there was no excuse whatsoever for literary criticism, cited two exceptions, or, if not exceptions to his basic notion, two men who wrote about literature and were worth reading on the subject: Hugh Kenner and Kenneth Cox, Cox being the more interesting of the two, at least as I inferred through the inflection in Bunting's voice. Kenner, raised in Ontario, I would already have heard of, not least as I was living and attending university in Canada at the time.

The next time I heard of Kenneth Cox was nearly ten years later when I was forwarded from the family home in New Jersey a literary magazine called *Montemora*, edited by a young Eliot Weinberger. In it were reviews by Cox of my 1978 Canadian collection of poems, *A Calendar of Airs*, and of Tom Pickard's 1979 collection, *Hero Dust*.

There was yet another review by Cox in that lively issue (the seventh in the magazine's estimable if too brief lifetime). This last was about Geoffrey Hill. It had previously been rejected by

William Cookson's magazine *Agenda*, effectively rupturing the relationship between Cox and Cookson. The former referred to the latter innumerable times in my presence as "that papist," spitting the term out with maximum plosive fury—and no small measure of relish.

Cox begins his essay on Hill thus: "Surely it cannot be denied Hill's work has many faults? And not accidental or occasional weaknesses but radical failings. His language is strained and if forcible also loose and even incorrect. Sensitive to certain tonal values it is deficient in statement and in organization."

Geoffrey Hill was very much regarded as a sacred cow in the precincts of *Agenda*, Cox's only significant outlet for his own criticism, and this act of sacrilege would not have been appreciated. Cox, for his part, was apoplectic that one of his essays was turned down because it skewered the reputation of one of the magazine's favorite contributors. You or I might have let it pass, given the circumstances, or not undertaken a project so sure to provoke a patron in the first place. Kenneth Cox was a singularly unaccommodating individual.

Agenda magazine was founded in 1959 by Cookson, then only twenty, after he'd had a long sit-down with Ezra Pound who, as was his wont, gave the youth a crash course in the fundamentals of the "Ezu-versity" curriculum. In the '70s and '80s, at least, and not infrequently before and after, it was one of the best and most influential literary magazines in the English language, particularly if one were interested in high modernism and its British exemplars, poets like Bunting, David Jones, and Hugh MacDiarmid. It still exists but has been irrelevant for many years, even before Cookson's death in 2003. I had visited Cookson in Battersea not long before his death in my capacity as a kind of diplomatic side channel, trying to negotiate a truce between Cox and Cookson, at least enough of one to get Cox's book of essays, *Collected Studies in the Use of English*, published by Agenda Editions.

Cookson, languid and affable in what I imagined to be the "toff" manner, with bookshelves groaning menacingly overhead, seemed to me not much less eccentric than Cox, whom I had by then visited a number of times in his Gunnersbury, Burlington Road flat. The scene felt to me, cultural outlander that I was, like the stage set of a 1930s drawing-room play or an Edwardian novel of manners, but my general ignorance, enthusiasm, and relative youth seem to have finally carried the day, and *Agenda* published the book in 2001, albeit at Cox's own expense. One of the finest books of literary essays in the modern era, it remains virtually unheard of. So does its author, though the 2016 posthumous collection, *The Art of Language*, may remedy that.

Cox was what one might call an amateur scholar, as opposed to the professional kind employed by universities. As pure writing—literature, if you will—his essays deserve to be read and reread as one would read those of William Hazlitt or Joseph Mitchell. They refresh and delight. They are a tonic for the mind and are best approached in the morning hours; one's entire day will be the better for it. Meanwhile, as proposition, explication, and argument of any given text, they are without equal. Models of clarity, concision, and insight, they make a mockery of almost all contemporaneous academic criticism, which next to Cox's essays seems fuzzy, ham-fisted, self-aggrandizing, tendentious, and dim. So it should come as no surprise that Cox has been completely ignored in academic circles, where his example would be of most use.

Kenneth Cox was born in London in 1916 and remained a Londoner throughout his long life, excepting travel as a young man and during his service in the Second World War. His father was a manager at a Cullen grocery. His mother was part Gypsy. It may have been due to his modest background that Cox was first drawn to communism and would remain a Marxist in sympathies, if never in doctrine, until his death. He almost never spoke of politics, so I was mildly surprised when he mentioned to me his political orientation. Nor are Marxist beliefs immediately apparent in his writings, apart from their revulsion for organized religion and a tendency toward extreme intellectual rigor in argument.

On the strength of that unusually keen intelligence, and through the offices of a sympathetic and observant teacher or two, Cox was allowed to attend London County Council schools in West Hampstead and then the University College School on Kingsgate Road. He briefly attended the University of London, but his temperament and highly individual cast of mind made him unsuited for further study in an institutional setting. Those

particular gifts were, however, put to good use in breaking en-
emy ciphers during the Second World War, when he worked as
a cryptographer in Cairo and Palestine. His success at breaking
codes, one very significant and seemingly impenetrable code in
particular, resulted in his being made an MBE after the war. He
was proud of this achievement, which was one of the very few
things he would allow to be noted with regard to his own life.
Otherwise, he sought and achieved almost complete invisibility
outside of his writings.

After the war, Cox tried his hand at bookselling for a time
but met with little success. He wound up working for the BBC,
a career employee in the Near Eastern Department, where his
task was to sift through that region's press and news broadcasts
for bits that might be relevant for BBC transmission. This em-
ployment lasted almost the entirety of his adult working life.
When he retired, his pension enabled him to live modestly but
comfortably in a flat near the Gunnersbury tube station in
southwest London on the District line, one stop from Kew Gardens, which we visited together one pleasant afternoon. His
family life appears to have been difficult, if not entirely miser-
able, including a wife who was committed to a mental institution and died there, and a son who grew up to become editor
of the main Newcastle daily newspaper, and who would die
young, estranged from his father.

I received a typed letter—most were handwritten—from
Cox in late summer 1997, which began as follows:

Dear August,

From your cat card I see you were to leave San Francisco for Jersey City on 9 August and from an earlier letter that you were then to go to Iowa City on the 14th. I will suppose this finds you settling in there but not yet acclimatised. Perhaps you will still be sorting out impressions attractions suspicions and similar innocent reactions to new surroundings. If you should have opened this letter while immersed in such matters may I suggest you stop reading it now. It is more suitable to be read in private and at leisure.

PAUSE

My only son Christopher died on 21 July aged 50. He leaves a widow and three children.

All three children are in their twenties, adult in law but each still in some degree dependent, none yet established in a congenial course of life. My daughter-in-law Pamela is however provided for and she has a job as well. A pleasant sensible energetic person, literate if not literary, she will become my heir and the executrix of my will. But she needs (indeed wants) somebody else to handle my writings (manuscripts correspondence notebooks copyrights) and dispose of my books. I should like you to take on that side of the work.

I'm not sure when I first began visiting Kenneth on my trips to London, but it had certainly become a part of my regular travel routine by the later 1990s and the first few years of this century. In a letter dated June 5, 1998, Cox, in a kind invitation, describes his abode:

> You may remember it boasts no guestroom and the small area not occupied by some 4000 books has to be shared with a pig-headed old man somewhat hard of hearing . . . Your sleeping place would consist of an old sofa which with a little effort can be transformed into a bed. Uncommon and perhaps unattractive to look at it provides a couch others beside myself have found more restful than usual. Space for your belongings is limited however and much of the time you would be living out of a suitcase. Access to bathroom is via my bedroom. But the place is quiet, warm enough and close to the main routes of travel.

Cox was a famously difficult and irascible man—a legend, really: everyone had stories—and more than a few might have characterized him, not entirely without cause, as *mad.* At the very least he would have seemed, to the casual observer, *eccentric.* I, personally, would suggest that he operated at a level of intensity that was well beyond the norm, and though assuredly odd, and often difficult, was by no means mentally imbalanced or *crazy,* at least not by the yardstick used for artists, writers, musicians, and the like. He was unfailingly courteous, warm, and hospitable toward me. Still, I was more than a little taken aback when he asked me to be his literary executor. I had visited at that point only two or three times. The more likely choice would have been his other young literary friend, the Lorine Niedecker scholar Jenny Penberthy, but he surmised, correctly, I'm sure, that between work and a young family, Jenny would be overburdened with other obligations. Most of those who might have been disposed toward taking him on Kenneth had already terminally alienated. Regarding him as a genius, I was startled to be asked, and, I suppose, rather flattered.

Even if he was well-disposed toward someone, as he seemed to be toward me, Kenneth was a formidable, sometimes intimidating presence to be alone in a room with, discussing literature and the life of the mind. He politely tolerated my own uninformed, half-baked remarks about this and that. I doubt they were of any real interest to him. At one point I decided to brave the observation that the closest model for the method and style of his essays seemed to be the nineteenth-century British naturalists. Under the circumstances, this involved no little temerity on my part. Cox regarded me closely for a few moments and in a manner I had not experienced from him previously. It made me uneasy, to be sure. Fortunately, my speculation turned out to be correct, and a very pleased Kenneth Cox later sent me his favorite passage from Alfred Russel Wallace's autobiography *My Life*, describing the author's fascination with the strange music and sensuous articulations of a linseed mill. The passage is at once richly detailed and uncongested, but, characteristically, Cox left it for me to divine what had pleased him about it.

A serious amateur philologist, Cox had at least a reading

knowledge of the Romance languages, along with Hungarian, Polish, Greek, and German. There would have been others of which he had cursory knowledge. He rendered into English a masterful version of Federigo Tozzi's novel *Con gli occhi chiusi* (published as *Eyes Shut* by Carcanet Press in 1990). Unpublished is an extended and brilliant translation of Leopardi's "II Parini, ovvero della Gloria" as "Parini on Fame." He translated from the Scots Gaelic, as well. He regretted never having written on Colette or Céline, both of whose writings he revered, particularly the former. The critic-as-philologist is everywhere evident throughout his critical writings.

Cox began publishing his essays in the late '60s in *Agenda* and the *Cambridge Quarterly*. The earliest dated essay in his new and revised collection is from 1966 and concerns the poetry of Basil Bunting. Cox was age fifty at the time. The thirty essays that make up the 2001 Agenda Editions collection are, but for two writers, Chaucer and Gissing, concerned with twentieth-century figures, chiefly but not exclusively modernist in approach. The presiding intellectual spirit behind the essays, and Cox's hero, is Ezra Pound, whom Cox came to physically resemble in his old age. He had particular feeling for the work of Basil Bunting and Louis Zukofsky, although he became somewhat disillusioned over time with the work of the latter. He seemed not to have cared personally very much for either man, at least in our conversations, though that is nowhere evident in his writings about Bunting. But outside of Pound,

Cox's most powerful feelings—which seemed to include genuine tenderness—were reserved for Lorine Niedecker and her poetry. Cox and Niedecker enjoyed an extensive and fascinating correspondence.

Collected Studies in the Use of English, an unusual but revealing title for a book of literary essays, can seem at times to resemble nothing so much as a naturalist's analysis of a series of specimens, classifying them by taxonomy: family, species, genus, order. Cox writes of his selections and method in the book's preface:

> Choice has been determined by personal inclination from among the materials available, chance discoveries and occasional recommendations.
>
> The outcome of search carried out by these means is emphasis on literature as the art of language. Attention is directed towards tone and movement and significance is drawn from these features as well as from overt meaning. Rigour of treatment tends to increase with the daring and ingenuity of the writing discussed.

Kenneth and I had a long correspondence. I received well over a hundred letters from him written over the course of about fifteen years. These letters have all the austere brilliance of style and acuity of observation of the critical prose. They could be very funny, or at least generously sprinkled with oblique and telling asperities. In many of the letters he is quite excited about a project at hand: essays on Gissing, Pound, Zukofsky, et al.

He would also share his thoughts on what he was reading at the time:

Am reading Edmund Wilson's *Patriotic gore* [*sic*] with immense respect and I hope some profit. The whole thing clearly seen throughout by dint alone of literary discrimination. How backwards, mudstuck even, do avantgardists in comparison appear.

Lichtenberg writes in appearance an ordinary style sped up a bit, so you have to look out for jumps, salvos, non-sequiturs and the like without breaking tone. He said himself he went (?came) to England to learn how to write German. I think had in mind that instinctive freedom of reference, of phrases of syntax you find in speakers concerned entirely with what they are saying, not how they are saying it.

Cox also mentioned books he was reading at the time but, as was his custom, without comment. One was Julius Sachs's 1906 *History of Botany (1530–1860)*. I picked up a copy the other day:

We may at present omit the numerous remarks on assimilation and the movement of the sap; the descriptions and figures of the parts of buds and of the course of the bundles of vessels in different parts of plants, and especially the analyses of the flower and fruit and the examination of the seed and embryo, conducted with a carefulness remarkable for that time, deserve a fuller notice, but this would detain us too long from our main subject.

Sachs is here writing about Malpighi and Grew's *Phytotomy Founded* (1671–1682). Cox, I'm certain, would have read that passage with pleasure.

In another of his letters, Cox writes:

> I didn't give a toss about the writer's state of mind, all I cared for was the play of words. I would go round savouring a phrase to test it, taste it, till I could decide it was 'good' or had to be spat out. That word taste is not a metaphor. People talk about the sound of language but the real thing is its taste, in the mouth, harsh sweet pungent, produced by the *movement* of sound.

Taste produced by movement—that was his test for his own work, as well as for that of the writers he admired. It links his views on the use of English from Joyce, Pound, and Niedecker, on the one hand, to Wallace and Sachs on the other. I learned a great deal from Cox's letters and not only from the art of them. To be the repository of so much observation and commentary from one of that quality of mind is, looking back, one of the treasures of my life.

The last time I visited Kenneth at his Burlington Road flat, he greeted me at the top of the steep flight of steps that led from street level to his front door and said to me, sotto voce and with some gravity, "August, there's someone I'd like you to meet." On entering the hallway, I saw a marvelously striking old woman seated by a table across the living room, smoking her cigarette and taking me in with a kind, welcoming smile. "August Kleinzahler," Kenneth said, with a formal flourish, "Lady Spender." And there she was, Natasha Spender, one of the great enchantresses of midcentury literary London.

It all seemed rather incongruous and unreal. What was she doing at Kenneth's book-laden, musty flat on Burlington Road? It would have been a far cry from the world of St. John's Wood where she and Stephen entertained for all those years, or Mas St. Jerome, the farmhouse in Provence. It occurred to me at the time, and since, that Kenneth would likely have despised Spender, the man and writer. Best as I could gather over the time I knew him, Kenneth had almost no visitors, or friends, for that matter. A couple of neighbor ladies would peek in every so often to see that he was all right, that's it. Natasha and Kenneth were not only friendly, they seemed to have been friendly for quite a long time, very friendly indeed, even a bit giggly together. Kenneth hardly spoke a word that afternoon but wore an exceedingly pleased look on his face, almost conspiratorial in nature.

He could at times be forlorn, even desperate, especially as he struggled late in life to find an outlet for his writing. But the gleam of mischief never guttered. Here is a letter to me dated January 22, 2003:

> Dear August,
>
> You sound restless, discontented. Nothing quite right or quite ready. Yet but one feels it ought to be. I tend to associate the mood with preverbal weather of the kind we get here but that's probably a local or personal trait. The distinguishing and

I would say dangerous feature is that it tends to promote optimism. The virulence of fallacy in circumstances apparently unpropitious is amazing. Consultation is the best remedy I know but you may have had better upbringing or traditional instruction. Oneself is not to be trusted, the little devil is too smart.

All the same I have good news which cannot be doubted: William Cookson is dead.

Kenneth died on March 4, 2005. Whatever the disappointments of his final years, he lived to see the publication of his book in 2001 and the death of Cookson two years later. I would be hard-pressed to say which of the two occasions gave him more pleasure.

ALASKA

In April 1973 I stepped off the *Wickersham*, flagship of the Alaska ferry system, and into the mud and rain of Juneau. I had come to make my fortune.

I was presently living on an abandoned wharf overlooking the Gastineau Channel about a mile south of town, below the old AJ Mine (the Alaska Juneau Gold Mining Mill, built in 1916). I had as a companion there another young wayfarer, Lincoln Hart from Grants Pass, Oregon, and in this I was most fortunate as he was knowledgeable about living out-of-doors, which I was, and am, not.

Lincoln and I had met briefly on the ferry as it headed north through the Inside Passage, weaving its way past the small, heavily forested islands and fjords. On encountering him again, only shortly after having disembarked, and then, subsequently, having been thrown off a fish boat in Harris Harbor where I'd enjoyed temporary lodging, Lincoln invited me to his secret kip at the "Seaside Marriott." It wasn't too bad out there on the wharf, really. We had mummy bags that kept us warm. Though open to the air on three sides, and facing out toward the water, with the lights of Douglas flickering a mile across the channel, there was a corrugated roof overhead and an empty oil drum where we could stow our gear. The police would come by every night about eleven and sweep their headlights across the wharf, but we were tucked well back and out of view.

Hundreds of young men just like us flooded into Juneau every spring hoping to get construction work or hop onto a fishing boat to take advantage of the inflated wages for semi- and unskilled labor available in Alaska in those days, and perhaps still. The North Slope pipeline had just begun construction that winter, employing thousands of young men in the far north, up by the Beaufort Sea. Many of them, along with the loggers and fishermen, would make their way down through Juneau at some point, filling the bars and spending their money, as carelessly as possible, or so it seemed to me, who was there to raise a stake and then travel to the south of Spain or Provence, dedicating myself to the writing of deathless verse and living on the cheap. I suspect I may well have been alone, among those many others, in having that particular ambition.

The word around town was: (1) The weather's going to break any day now, and (2) there'll be so much work in two weeks' time that they'll be dragging useless bastards like you off the street and paying you fourteen dollars an hour, which was big money in those days.

The weather never broke, not the entire nine months I was there. And no one was dragging anyone off the street to work for fourteen dollars an hour, not even for half that. In fact, there was no dragging whatsoever, except maybe outside this bar or that on Franklin Street late Saturday nights.

By the time Memorial Day had come and gone, the tide of

aspiring young workers from the "lower forty-eight" had receded dramatically. Lincoln and I, however, were paying "the nice price" at the Seaside Marriott and had managed to get food stamps from the government office downtown, which we supplemented with free peanuts every night at the Red Dog Saloon, where the tradesmen would often stand us drinks, most amused and impressed by Lincoln's and my al fresco lifestyle down there on the pier.

Every morning Lincoln and I, after being rudely awakened by some tour boat coming up the harbor and blasting its horns at six o'clock, would make our way into town, stopping first at the Franklin Hotel. We had a friend named John, a recent graduate of Vassar, among the first male alumni, who had set himself up at the hotel because he needed a "clean" place for his daily insulin injections. Lincoln and I kept a few personal belongings with John and spent our Sundays there in his small room, with everything shut down in town except the bars, reading and rereading the weekend edition of the *Seattle Post-Intelligencer*, which we all chipped in to buy. As was always the case, it would be pouring down rain outside, cold rain. The walls of John's room were riddled with bullet holes. The toilet in the hall would have made a mendicant from Calcutta blanch. And in the stairwell dwelt a woman of indeterminate age screaming, "Fuck me, fuck me," all day and well into the evening.

The next stop for Lincoln and me was the doughnut shop for coffee and a bite. Then we'd head to the State Office Building, which had a library and an enormous old-fashioned lavatory where we'd strip down to our jeans and wash up, best as we could, in the big basins on offer. There was a public pay shower in town where we'd clean ourselves up properly a couple of days a week. If a suit walked into the lavatory while Lincoln and I were at our ablutions, we might catch a funny look but never a reprimand. Juneau was that sort of place back then.

Lincoln would then, at eight a.m., proceed to the carpenters' union hall. He'd worked green chain at an Oregon sawmill and his Lumber & Sawmill Workers union card looked a fair bit like a Juneau Carpenters & Joiners card, enough at least so he managed to pass. The Manpower office opened an hour later, so I'd hang out at the State Library reading back issues of *The Spectator* to kill time (don't ask me what *The Spectator* was doing there). I spent so much time reading through the back issues from the '60s and early '70s that I not only assimilated the magazine's house style but also became conversant with all manner of gossip and opinionating from literary Britain of that era.

Lincoln didn't manage to get any work out of the hall those first couple of months, and I seldom got lucky at Manpower. Such was the work—cleaning up somebody else's big mess, laying concrete foundations on a hillside in the rain—that I was never particularly sorry when I didn't, much as I needed the money. So by about ten every morning Lincoln and I would hook up at the Municipal Library, an old-fashioned Andrew Carnegie sort of affair a block from the State Library; it had three rooms, and in one of them—named the Alaskan Room— was a couch. We would spend most of our waking hours there, six days a week, all day, with the rain pouring down. Lincoln read carpentry books, especially *Modern Carpentry* by Willis Wagner, as he didn't really know much about the subject. Doors, the hanging of, and staircases and the challenges they presented especially drew his attention, as I recall. For my part, I pursued my usual desultory, heterogeneous fare: essays, travel books, James M. Cain, Ross Macdonald, poetry, back issues of *Harper's, The Atlantic, The New Yorker.*

There were several librarians, and they all disapproved of Lincoln and me having set up residence at the library, in varying degrees, except one, Dale DeArmond, an older woman who had worked as a city librarian in Juneau since 1958. She would retire six years later. I'd later learn that Ms. DeArmond was a noted woodcut artist and children's book illustrator; in fact, she has an entry in *Contemporary Authors* in which, in answer to the question about her politics she replies, "Liberal, sort of"; and to the question about her religion, "Agnostic." Both answers would have raised suspicions in the Juneau of that era, not because they seemed extreme in any way but because they would have looked rather exotic in a town where the mind-set lurched from Anarcho-Syndicalist to Nativist Dada to antediluvian, pistol-packing, God-fearing secessionists waving the old Alaska Territory flag with its eight gold stars against a field of dark blue, representing the Big Dipper and the North Star. I like to think that Ms. DeArmond spotted Lincoln and me as a couple of enlightened young gents temporarily down on their luck. In any event, when she was manning the front desk, Lincoln and I got to take turns cutting some zzzz's on that couch in the Alaskan Room.

Finally, one day in June, Lincoln got out of the Union Hall with work up the road at a new development near the Mendenhall Glacier. I, meanwhile, had taken a job teaching a couple of nights a week at the University of Alaska, Juneau Extension: Buddhism, if you can imagine, and Creative Writing. One of my Buddhism students was a sixtyish, white-haired woman named Nancy, who had an extremely sardonic and un-Buddha-like manner, and who, it turned out, was drawn to strays. Upon learning of my circumstances on the wharf (where I now dwelt solo, Lincoln having moved nearer his job and brought his girlfriend to town), Nancy invited me to live in her big house at the top of a steep hill on West 7th Street, a large, one might even say grand, turn-of-the-century frame structure, with her husband, "Sweetie," a tall, nice-looking man a good deal younger than Nancy, with wavy hair and a handlebar mustache, who worked as a linesman and listened to Rod McKuen records after he got home in the evenings to relax, as well as her son by a previous relationship, Michael, who was my age. Also on hand was a vicious Belgian shepherd named Choctaw who was generally kept behind French doors in the parlor except when Michael took him out for a walk, and a schizophrenic cat named Baby Teapot with her own bedroom upstairs, which only Nancy was allowed to visit: the cat like some deranged old aunt hidden away upstairs in a southern Gothic novel. I was dispatched straightaway to a cavernous, unheated attic, where I bedded down every evening on the floor in my mummy bag with one of the most extraordinary views I've ever enjoyed, looking south across the Juneau flats, the Gastineau Channel with the barges and tour boats passing in and out, and to the west Mt. Jumbo, mist climbing it like a fifteenth-century Japanese ink drawing or a Sung Dynasty landscape.

I lived for seven months in that house, rent-free, well fed, and properly looked after. It was probably the greatest kindness shown to me in this life, and my first little chapbook, published four years later in Montreal, is dedicated to "Nancy Dethridge, the Belle of Juneau."

Nancy would never take a dime from me, even after making a phone call a few days after I had moved in, finding me a job at the Alaska State Museum. It wasn't fourteen dollars an hour, but it was a job, and a very fine job, I quickly realized. Nancy, it turned out, had more juice in town than Gloria Vanderbilt, Brooke Astor, and Dorothy Schiff combined. She had a direct line to the chief of police, the editor of the local newspaper, *The Southeast Alaskan Empire*, the director of the animal shelter, you name it. And whatever Nancy didn't get wind of first, her friend Peggy, who ran the florist shop, had covered, her bailiwick primarily the realm of sexual impropriety. If Juneau had an un-official religion, it would have been the Church of Alcohol and Fornication, and Peggy was the high priestess of the latter, at least insofar as keeping tabs. Running a flower shop is not a bad way to track such things.

As regards alcohol, Juneau was named in 1881 after a French-

Canadian prospector and drunkard named Joe Juneau. The word "hooch" is derived from Hoochinoo, the name of a Tlingit tribe known for brewing their own variety of moonshine.

The best-attended church for the worship of Alcohol and Fornication was a Filipino dance bar called Dreamland down near the southern edge of town. It was open only on Friday and Saturday nights, from around ten p.m. until four or so in the morning. During summer, it was light when you walked in and light when you staggered out. There were quite a few knifings in there. Mike had warned me before my first visit to Dreamland not to engage the eyes of any of the Filipino men. Not everyone was privy to that wisdom. One would hear, during the course of any given evening, the thud of bodies hitting the floor at irregular intervals, followed by piteous groaning. The house band was called Melange, which most of those in attendance, with questionable knowledge of French, thought meant ménage à trois. There were about ten men for every woman in Juneau back then. Rain and mud notwithstanding, it was the best of places to be a girl.

One of my motivations for signing up to teach a couple of extension courses was to find a tolerable job and living situation, which I had now succeeded in doing, and to meet girls, which didn't turn out terribly well. I did, in fact, have a girlfriend at the time, after a fashion, who would torture me with long letters from Paris about the importunings of her amorous employer, for whom she worked as an au pair. I had only one "official" date in all my months in Juneau; we went out one Saturday night to see

The Godfather, if I'm not mistaken, which had come to Juneau a curiously long time after its initial release. I had invited one of my students, a beautiful Tlingit woman, a few years older than I, a little rough around the edges and with a couple of small children out of wedlock. Her name was Doloresa "Yelling Sea Water." Doloresa, it turned out, arrived late that evening as I waited impatiently in front of the theater in the rain. But she did finally turn up, in white go-go boots and a very mini miniskirt. The theater was already packed, the only seats left in the front row. It seemed like all two hundred people in attendance, not a few of whom I knew, Juneau being a not very big town, were checking Doloresa and me out as we sheepishly made our way to the front. At least *I* felt sheepish . . . As we sat down the lights began to dim, the curtains to part. The audience fell silent, and just then Doloresa turned to me, suddenly indignant, roaring, "How about some fucking popcorn, Gus!?"

ROY FISHER

In a 1979 review of Roy Fisher's collection of poems *The Thing about Joe Sullivan*, probably the most likable collection by a not always likable poet, John Ash wrote: "In a better world, he would be as widely known and highly praised as Ted Hughes and Seamus Heaney." This would be a very strange world, and not necessarily a better one. Fisher has never aspired to the sort of readership that Heaney and Hughes enjoy; it's not clear he has aspired to much of a readership at all. Astringent in tone, the voice denuded of personality, and with all the warmth of a lens—exploratory, restless, difficult—it is poetry almost entirely without charm. On first learning that his work was being read outside a small circle of poet friends, Fisher froze up for an extended period of time, as he would periodically throughout his writing life. There isn't much in his poetry that would provide fuel for the more significant engines of reputation. It is too heterodox in form and method, and too various to characterize or place comfortably in the context of contemporary British poetry, beyond the idiotic and self-marginalizing labels of "outsider" or "experimental."

A poem, Fisher said in an interview, "has business to exist . . . if there's a reasonable chance that somebody may have his perceptions rearranged by having read it." The poem exists as "a subversive agent, psychologically, sensuously, however you like." The aim is to produce a dislocative effect. "I'm very suspicious of poetry which can be embraced by people who are interested in, as it were, identifying a culture as a culture at a particular moment."

All of this may sound appealingly provocative and avant-garde, but in practice it puts off most readers and jettisons what small prospects exist for serious critical reception. But Fisher throughout his career has learned and taken advantage of "what it is possible to do, freed from readership."

"I come from the thing called the 'working class,'" he says, "and I didn't go to one of the older universities, and I've never lived in London. I'm a provincial . . . Which is everywhere but London and Oxford and Cambridge, and one or two rather well-to-do spots around that way. It doesn't mean much, but it affects the way you behave, and what you root for and what you snarl at." A lifelong, rather cheerful agoraphobe and hermit, neglect suits him. Nevertheless, *The Long and the Short of It*, published in Fisher's seventy-fifth year, should find a substantial readership beyond the poets and scholars who have constituted his audience from the beginning. As the difficulties and intellectual prejudices abate, the more significant poems will almost certainly make their way into the canon.

The title poem in the 1978 collection that Ash so rightly praised, "The Thing about Joe Sullivan," written in 1975, is terrifically bracing and approachable, in its defiant way, and could be read as Fisher's ars poetica. Fisher has worked as a professional jazz pianist throughout his life. He was a musician before he was a poet, and music has probably meant more to him than poetry. Fisher likes no jazz pianist more than Joe Sullivan, the rumbustious white Chicago artist who came up in the 1920s with Eddie Condon's band. Like Fisher, Sullivan was an unabashed disciple of the Earl Hines style of playing, with that busily inventive left hand and the right hand playing octaves:

> The pianist Joe Sullivan,
> jamming sound against idea
>
> hard as it can go
> florid and dangerous
>
> slams at the beat, or hovers,
> drumming, along its spikes

Farther along:

> For all that, he won't swing
> like all the others;
>
> disregards mere continuity,
> the snakecharming business,
>
> the "masturbator's rhythm"
> under the long variations

And then:

> The mannerism of intensity
> often with him seems true,

too much to be said, the mood
pressing in right at the start, then

running among stock forms
that could play themselves

and moving there with such
quickness of intellect

that shapes flaw and fuse,
altering without much sign

It concludes with the poet/pianist attempting a Sullivan solo on
his own piano:

. . . fingers following his
through figures that sound obvious

find corners everywhere,
marks of invention, wakefulness;

the rapid and perverse
tracks that ordinary feelings

make when they get driven
hard enough against time.

This is an anomalous poem for Fisher, and a splendid one: an
anthology piece, and one of the very few first-rate poems about
jazz. "I'm not interested in making a structure which has got a
climax, a thing which has got an authoritarian centre, a rule or

mandate somewhere in its middle which the work will unfold and will reach." Except when he is, as in this poem.

And then there is his most commonly anthologized piece, "The Entertainment of War," about the bombing of his native Birmingham during the Second World War:

> A mile away in the night I had heard the bombs
> Sing and then burst themselves between cramped houses
> With bright soft flashes and sounds like banging doors;
>
> The last of them crushed the four bodies into the ground,
> Scattered the shelter, and blasted my uncle's corpse
> Over the housetop and into the street beyond.

This poem, again, is unusual: Fisher is almost never autobiographical, interested in narrative, or inclined to relate "brute documentary." Nor is there often a stable, identifiable "I": "My poems are propositions or explorations rather than reactions to personal experience," he says. "The poems are to do with getting about in the mind . . . from one cluster of ideas to another without a scaffolding of logic or narrative . . . the way a poem moves is the index of where the feeling in it lies." In "Of the Empirical Self and for Me" he writes:

> In my poems there's seldom
> any *I* or *you*—
>
> you know me, Mary;
> you wouldn't expect it of me—

"The Entertainment of War" is part of an "assemblage" of poems titled *City* (1961) that Fisher started to write about Birmingham when he returned there after a spell in the early 1950s in Devon, where he had lived with his first wife and taught at a grammar school. Fisher had lived in a single house in Birmingham until he was twenty-three, never traveling far afield or for any length of time. On his return to the area, he landed a job at a teacher-training college and set up house in Handsworth, only a few hundred yards from the house in which his mother had been raised. Fisher supplemented his income by working most nights "playing in Dixieland bands, bebop quartets and Black Country dance bands; for a while I was the token white in the Andy Hamilton Caribbean Combo." He played in jazz clubs, town halls, village halls, strip clubs, dance halls, drinking clubs, and hotels. None of this work finds its way into the poetry, at least directly, but being away from Birmingham for so long had given him an artistic distance from it. "My journeys through it in connection with my educational work and my piano playing were in all directions at all hours of the day and night. I saw it from the oddest of angles."

While in Devon, Fisher had been reading, looking at, and listening to the important moderns and had begun publishing his own poems. As was, and remains, his custom, he nosed about on his own. One early non-Modernist influence was Robert Graves, and the "brusque conversational tone" in some of his poetry. In the mid-1950s, the poet Gael Turnbull, who was editing a special British number for Cid Corman's magazine *Ori-*

gin, took an interest in Fisher's work and invited him to his home in Worcester. There, Fisher saw for the first time the work of the later William Carlos Williams, Basil Bunting, Robert Duncan, Allen Ginsberg, Louis Zukofsky, Robert Creeley, Charles Olson, and others. "I'd never seen poetry used as these people were, in their various ways, using it," Fisher remembered, "nor had I seen it treated as so vital an activity. These people were behaving with all the freedom and artistic optimism of painters. Decidedly un-English." *The Long and the Short of It* is dedicated to Turnbull, as well as to Fisher's late second wife, the playwright Joyce Holliday.

Had Fisher continued to write poetry in the vein of "The Thing about Joe Sullivan" and "The Entertainment of War," he might well have enjoyed a proper career. But the method of much of the writing, even in *City*, assured him of marginality, at best. *City's* subject matter is urban, the technique a blend of the surreal, expressionist, realist, and cubist, the whole thing almost cinematic in its abrupt transitions and dislocations. In fact, the sort of thing you see every day on TV adverts or in front of your nose on Tottenham Court Road or Oxford Street. Fisher's reading of it—on a vinyl recording he made for the tiny Amber label in 1977—sounds almost like the voice-over to a documentary or an exhibition of photojournalism: an unusually artful, strange, and dissociative documentary or exhibit, to be sure, and one that could be shot only in black and white. Fisher's poetry, almost all of it, occurs in a crepuscular world of halftones and chiaroscuro:

Brick-dust in sunlight. That is what I see now in the city, a dry epic flavour, whose air is human breath. A place of walls made straight with plumbline and trowel, to desiccate and crumble in the sun and smoke. Blistered paint on cisterns and girders, cracking to show the priming. Old men spit on the paving slabs, little boys urinate; and the sun dries it as it dries out patches of damp on plaster facings to leave misshapen stains. I look for things here that make old men and dead men seem young. Things which have escaped, the landscapes of many childhoods.

Wharves, the oldest parts of factories, tarred gable ends rearing to take the sun over lower roofs. Soot, sunlight, brick-dust; and the breath that tastes of them.

There's that sort of thing, but there's also this:

At night on the station platform, near a pile of baskets, a couple embraced, pressed close together and swaying a little. It was hard to see where the girl's feet and legs were. The suspicion this aroused soon caused her hands, apparently joined behind her lover's back, to become a small brown paper parcel under the arm of a stout engine-driver who leaned, probably drunk, against the baskets, his cap so far forward as almost to conceal his face. I could not banish the thought that what I had first seen was in fact his own androgynous fantasy, the self-sufficient core of his stupor. Such a romantic thing, so tender, for him to contain. He looked more comic and complaisant than the couple had done, and more likely to fall heavily to the floor.

The prose alternates with verse. As Kenneth Cox said in one of the very few useful pieces on Fisher's poetry, the verse line slows down the rate of reading and highlights details of movement and texture, as well as allowing a more flexible syntax and looser connections between successive meanings:

> The sun hacks at the slaughterhouse campanile,
> And by the butchers' cars, packed tail-to-kerb,
> Masks under white caps wake into human faces.
>
> The river shudders as dawn drums on its culvert;
> On the first bus nightworkers sleep, or stare
> At hoardings that look out on yesterday.
>
> The whale-back hill assumes its concrete city:
> The white-flanked towers, the stillborn monuments;
> The thousand golden offices, untenanted.

It's a temptation for critics who write about the early work to get caught up in its bleak, social-realist aspect. In a review of Fisher's 1968 *Collected* from Fulcrum Press, Donald Davie found strong affinities between Fisher and Larkin, in particular the "piercing pathos" and the way that Fisher restricts "himself as self-denyingly as Larkin to the urbanised and industrialised landscapes of modern England." Davie goes on to align both poets in the tradition of Thomas Hardy. Jacques Réda and *Les Ruines de Paris* would seem the safer bet, along with the urban photography of Bill Brandt; but all bets are finally off with Fisher, so wide and unpredictable are his influences, and so diffused.

Most of the lineaments of Fisher's mature work are already present in *City*, however, a remarkable achievement for a writer in his twenties. He sets out to write about an actual city but to "dissolve" its particulars and make them strange until it becomes as much an inner perceptual field as a postindustrial Midlands wasteland.

"I always assume," Fisher said in an interview, that "I can handle subtleties, velleities, half-tones, but not anything brash. Had I been a painter I'd have needed slaves to mix my colours, for the sight of reds, yellows and blacks splurging aggressively from the tubes would have wrecked me for the day." These halftones are nowhere more in evidence or handled more masterfully than in "Metamorphoses," a 1970 prose poem:

> She sleeps, in the day, in the silence. Where there is light, but little else: the white covers, the pillow, her head with its ordinary hair, her forearm dark over the sheet.

> She sleeps and it is hardly a mark on the stillness; that she should have moved to be there, that she should be moving now across her sleep as the window where the light comes in passes across the day.

> Her warmth is in the shadows of the bed, and the bed has few shadows, the sky is smoked with a little cloud, there are fish-trails high in the air. Her sleep rides on the silence, it is an open mouth travelling backward on moving waves.

Mouth open across the water, the knees loosened in sleep; dusks of the body shadowed around the room. In the light from the windows there is the thought of a beat, a flicker, an alternation of aspect from the outside to the inside of the glass. The light is going deep under her.

The poem isn't about anything in particular; very few Fisher poems are. You don't know where you are or who's on board. The metamorphoses are tonal and proceed glacially, like the massive tone clusters of a Ligeti orchestral piece.

Red beans in to soak. A thickness of them, almost brimming to the glass basin, swelling and softening together, the colour of their husks draining out to a fog of blood in the water.

The mass of things, indistinguishable one from another, loosing their qualities into the common cloud, their depth squashed by the refraction and obscured in the stain, forms pushed out of line. Five beans down it may be different.

"Metamorphoses" is far more representative of what Fisher is about than "The Thing about Joe Sullivan" or "The Entertainment of War," but it would be a very hard sell to whoever's putting together the next *Oxford Book of Twentieth-Century British Verse*.

"There's little poetry in my head," Fisher says, "which is filled instead with almost continuous music and optical polaroids." It's almost exclusively these that get into the poetry, black and white, often out of focus, the images scrambled, their tonal qualities different from one another. As a child Fisher was a gifted painter. That went by the board in his teens and was supplanted by jazz, but it's the visual that dominates the perceptual field of his poetry. Fisher claims to have been blessed, or cursed, with near photographic recall, and there is throughout the poetry a fetishizing of remembered images.

"Metamorphoses" was written later, the same year as "The Cut Pages," sixteen pages of wildly disjunct and spontaneous outpourings that began as an exercise to break out from a long period of not writing and personal crisis. The poem is more anomalous in its freedom than "The Entertainment of War" in its containment:

> Korean chrysanthemum, flattened into a fan. Rushing in,
>   seeing it,
> falling on his knees, struggling on his knees to justify it
>
> He must have come from somewhere. Terra Cotta Brick
>
> Sham signifiers, wearing the palms bearing the bays, keeping
>   the places patrolled,
> walking the dogs' dogs. There seems to be
>
> British Bakelite could rise again

And so on. Those who have followed Fisher's work closely—very closely—will recognize the fetishized imagery (brick), the cadences, the way Fisher's mind moves. This last feature would make it most identifiable to me, at least in a blind test. Predictably, I suppose, Marjorie Perloff, in an admiring essay, thinks "The Cut Pages" is the best thing Fisher has ever done, is the reason he was put on this planet: a precursor to the so-called L=A=N=G=U=A=G=E poets. Perloff is not entirely wrong, except that the poem is of little interest except to the most specialized, and tolerant, reader.

Fisher's poetry abounds with detours and experiments, which even if unsuccessful open entire new areas for him. "Matrix" and a number of other significant poems followed on the heels of "The Cut Pages," which Fisher prefers to call an "improvisation" rather than an "experiment": an attempt at "working as closely as I could to the elements of my language and its immediate fields of association, well below the levels of models that imaged the self and its extensions." Another significant and immeasurably more successful detour was "The Ship's Orchestra," written in 1962–1963. It is a surreally inflected twenty-two-page fantasia about an imaginary jazz band aboard an imaginary ship on an imaginary journey; it's identifiably Fisher, but again unlike anything else he's written:

> Then it was her black (purple, juice) net dress, rough to the touch, things grew so big in the dark. Or lacquered hair, dry and crisp as grey grass. Want it to come away in handfuls, and she be meek, and satisfied, as far as that. Plimsolls, the smell of feet in a boy's gymnasium. Learn to live with it.

> Merrett calls his saxophone a tusk. What shape is the field of vision the eyes experience? Its edges cannot be perceived. A pear-shape, filled with the white plastic tusk, rimmed and

ringed and keyed with snarly glitters, floating importantly. Where? Against a high, metallic and misty sunset, the sky like Canada in thaw, and Billy Budd's feet dangling out of heaven five miles up, through a long purplish cloud.

The piece feels almost as though the poet had fallen asleep during a break between sets with a copy of Burroughs's *Naked Lunch* spread across his face. Fisher had not yet read Burroughs, but there can't have been much of this sort of thing going down in Handsworth in 1961.

The eye darts about in Fisher's poetry. It abhors the object at rest, framing of any kind. It's like a camera jerking and swiveling on an unstable tripod. Early and late, the poetry is about the eye in motion. The shifts may be subtle or vertiginously abrupt. It's best not to get too comfortable as you progress through a poem because you're not going to be where you think you are for long:

> From here to there—
> a trip between two locations
> ill-conceived, raw, surreal
> outgrowths of common sense, almost
> merging one into the other
>
> except for the turn
> where here and there
> change places, the moment
> always a surprise:

on an ordinary day a brief

lightness, charm between realities;

on a good day, a break

life can flood in and fill.

("Handsworth Liberties")

Roy Fisher's publishing history has been a mess, as it customarily is for those poets consigned to the margins who have managed to persist at their art over many years. *The Long and the Short of It* is, effectively, his fourth "Collected Poems." The first came from Fulcrum in 1968. Fisher supposed, at the time, that he'd gathered together what he wanted in print or was capable of, and was leaving all that foolishness behind. Not to be. He later had two collecteds from Oxford: *Poems: 1955–80* (1980) and *Poems 1955–87* (1987). His new collection and *The Dow Low Drop: New and Selected Poems* (1997) are from Bloodaxe. Pretty much everything is here in this new volume. It's not chronologically arranged, which is a minor nuisance to the reviewer but not to the reader. (The poems are all dated in the index.) The poet tells us in the acknowledgments: "These poems no more amount to a biography than I do; and my habits of working on projects from time to time over long periods and my heterodox approach to methods I use would make an arrangement that seemed chronological false: so nothing of the kind is here attempted." Stick that in your pipe and smoke it.

His masterwork, *A Furnace*, was issued by Oxford in 1986. Again, it is recognizably Fisher but not at all like anything else he'd written. Dedicated to John Cowper Powys, who would seem at first glance an unlikely model for the poet, it is a fifty-seven-page, thirteen-hundred-plus-line composition in seven parts, an excavation of a site through time, conflating the local aluminum works, John Dee, the Neolithic spirit world, Great-Grandfather William, Adolphe Sax, modern Chicago, the transit of Augusta Treverorum to Trier, and old rocks of every description, all of it glued together with a very loose, homemade animism. It is Fisher's richest and most challenging poem, and one that requires many readings over time to unwind the elaborate braiding of its elements.

Fisher now lives in "that strange miniaturized mountain landscape at the edge of the Derbyshire limestone, where green conical hills shoot up fantastically hundreds of feet from the banks of the upper Dove." Birmingham isn't far, however; it never is.

HOW I BECAME

A MUSIC CRITIC

Then there was the time I sold all my CDs. Well, not all of them. I kept seventy-five. I had twenty-five hundred CDs spread out over ten big shelves, and not one of them did I wish to part with. Which may sound extreme, but bear in mind that those ten shelves represented several years of exhaustive sifting and winnowing through thousands of other CDs, less critical to my listening pleasure and notions of the indispensable. So when I picked out my ten or fifteen CDs a day to take down to Recycled Records on Haight Street for four or five bucks apiece, I was separating myself, more painfully by the day, first from my darlings, then my darlingest of darlings. At the end of this self-inflicted ordeal, I came to know vividly what music I cared most to have on hand.

You see, I was broke. My *lifestylesoftherichandfamous* routine had deteriorated to oh, dearie me, how am I going to pay rent *and* that Pacific Gas & Electric bill. I had no one to blame but myself. I had forgotten to find a job, having instead been listening to music and making tapes—for years. I'd won a grant, a fellowship, a very generous one, perhaps deserved, perhaps not, who cares? Regardless, I spent all my money on CDs, and all my time listening to them. I am a feckless fellow. Go ahead, say it. I shan't argue. "Never argue with a liar or a fool," my grandfather used to say. Am I calling you a liar or a fool? Your spouse might. Your adversary might. Not I. Simply, I shall not defend my lifestyle from you or anyone else.

I had no *things*. I have more *things* today, but still not many. Then, I had almost no *things* whatsoever. In those days my existence was rather peripatetic and I was living in a rent-controlled flat, the same one I live in now. But now I have a wife, so along with dresses and brassieres and bath oils there are more *things*. Then, not—neither wife nor things. I had books. I had music. Most of my books I wound up selling to secondhand booksellers, at least those that were resalable. Fortunately, most of the books that meant the most to me were of no interest to anyone else. My furniture was crap. It still is. Ask my wife. No computer or printer or microwave. The TV was a ten-inch black-and-white Panasonic an old girlfriend had been given for her college graduation in 1977. This is 1995 I'm talking. Everyone on the TV looked like coneheads, which pleased me. Besides, there was nothing on TV, then or now, apart from a ball game or some particularly lurid segment from *Hard Copy* or *Entertainment Tonight*. Another ex-girlfriend had left me an old VCR, but it wasn't compatible with the TV so I gave it away. What else can't people live without? A car? A John Deere tractor? I still don't have a car, tractor neither.

I got myself into the pickle innocently enough, what with the prize money. I quit my job at the lock shop; straight off I did that—*adios.* Sometime before that I had inherited a little CD player from the VCR girlfriend. She'd gotten it for signing up with a credit-card company. I had been dead set against CDs. I decided the record companies were jamming the new technology down our throats. But never you mind.

For some years up to that point I had been going to a used-record store out on the avenues, next to a vacuum cleaner repair shop. The owner was a rather gruff, taciturn fellow, but he knew a world about jazz and endured my questions over the years, questions like a four-year-old asks: "What's that?" "Who's that?" It must have been very annoying, and he started out somewhat grudging, but turned out to be a voluble, likable guy, at least regarding the subject of music—even with a callow thirty-something like myself.

It can be mighty quiet on a foggy Tuesday afternoon out there by 20th and Lincoln, just off the park, with the barber on the other side of the parking lot rereading the *Chronicle* sports section and the elderly in the Kentucky Fried Chicken next door lingering over their coffee. But for ten years before my CD phase, I went to school, as it were, out there at that record store, and learned a fair bit from Tom. That was his name, still is: Tom Madden. Never asked if he was related to the football coach. And before that I'd hang out at a small used-record shop just down the block here on Frederick Street where I live. A place called the Magic Flute, run by a guy named Flynn. I liked Flynn. He'd get this cheerful, marmoreal look on him when he was drunk, which was most of the time. I heard a lot of wonderful stuff in there, as well. I think it was in those earlier days at the Magic Flute that I began buying LPs and making tapes.

Comparison, like imitation, is a matchless instructional tool so far as the acquisition of knowledge is concerned, whether about partitas, bagels, or gearboxes. To tape, one after another, piano concerti by Gubaidulina, Lutosławski, Schnittke, Blacher, and Elliott Carter, to play that tape again and again, is to learn a great deal about the post-Bartókian concerto form. Likewise, to tape songs with extended bass solos by Jimmy Blanton, Oscar Pettiford, Mingus, Ray Brown, Scott LaFaro, and Paul Chambers is to learn not only the techniques and merits of the individual players but also the nature of the instrument, its expressive range, the role of the bass in ensemble playing— as well as picking up some other fundamentals, such as tonal color and rhythm. One's ears grow bigger with each listening, even if much of the knowledge comes in half consciously or even unconsciously.

CDs and CD players were made for taping, that was clear from the get-go. No fussing with getting the needle in the groove just right between plays, whether they are tunes, orchestral movements, birdcalls from the Carpathian forests, whathaveyou. Not to mention crackles, hisses, and pops. Just hit Pause and Bob's your uncle. I somehow overcame what I regarded as my principled Luddite objections (not for the first time, or last). Be that as it may, I got hold of one of my normal guy friends to come over and connect everything up for me, CD player, tape deck, receiver. Thus it began, my descent into musomania and, finally, penury.

As addictions go, it was quite marvelous, really. I didn't damage my health at all. It was expensive, certainly, but I was able to defray the costs through trades at secondhand places where the clerks knew me and let me exchange discs for only a couple of dollars or even-up, so that the stores became something like the equivalent of branch libraries. I pored over liner notes and books like Nicolas Slonimsky's *The Concise Baker's Biographical Dictionary of Musicians*, an extraordinary compendium worth reading even if you have no interest in classical or what's sometimes called "art music." Here is Slonimsky on Herbert von Karajan, the great German conductor and monster:

> He practiced yoga and aerobics, and for a while embraced Zen Buddhism. Moreover, he was known to believe in the transmigration of souls, and expressed a hope of being reborn as an eagle soaring above the Alps, his favorite mountain range. As an alternative, he investigated the technique of cryogenics, hoping that his body could be thawed a century or so later to enable him to enjoy yet another physical incarnation. None of these endeavors prevented him from being overcome by a sudden heart attack in his home at Anif in the Austrian Alps. A helicopter with a medical staff was quickly summoned to fly him to a hospital, but it arrived too late.

Collecting takes on a life of its own after a while, quite apart from the pleasures of listening. A not entirely wholesome appetite begins to assert itself at some point and along with it something like pridefulness, a lust for acquisition, covetousness. One has a *collection*. Friends would walk into the room off the hall with the shelves of music and remark, "Holy shit." It became part of my identity. "Have you checked out August's CD collection lately?" Blues, jazz, classical, world, R&B, bluegrass, country—one splendid disc (probably not easy to come by) after another. I considered willing them to a private institution of higher learning on my demise: the "Kleinzahler Collection" in a soundproofed chamber of the library at a small, elite liberal arts college in New England, with grateful, reverential students and faculty padding around, picking out discs and muttering under their breaths, "Wow," taken aback by my knowledge and flawless taste, my breathtaking hipness and magnanimity.

At one point I sold fifteen hundred CDs at a pop, when I was really squeezed for dough. The owner from Recycled came up to the flat with a few boxes and gave me a check. Before the week was over he'd sold the lot of them. He was, and remains, delighted with me.

When I returned to my apartment here in San Francisco after being on the road for a couple of years, I went through the assorted living-room drawers, which contained hundreds and hundreds of tapes, all carefully described: *Roland Kirk on Mercury (sans flute), Extra-Raffiné; Old Wien mit Schlag; Longhair Percussion Discussion; Mondo Bongo; Lento Cello Deluxe; Twelve Versions of "On Green Dolphin Street,"* etc. It occurred to me that the degree of concentrated toil and fascination on exhibit before me was not necessarily admirable but perhaps a bit obsessive, even morbid. Then again, over those few years of making my tapes and assembling my mighty CD collection, I acquainted myself with all manner of music and individual sounds: bebop tuba, Trautonium (a bit like a theremin), Aeolian harp, Raoul Hausmann and Kurt Schwitters, Screamin' Jay Hawkins, and Ivor Cutler . . . A world of useless, disconnected, auditory information—and then, one evening, after three years of collecting, the phone rang.

LORINE NIEDECKER

Well, I'll start with where born which is no doubt where I'll end—a section of low land on the Rock River where it empties into Lake Koshkonong, all near Fort Atkinson, Wisconsin. Nature is lush here, I feel as tho I spent my childhood outdoors— redwinged blackbirds, willows, maples, boats, fishing (the smell of tarred nets), tittering and squawking noises from the marsh, a happy, outdoor grandfather who somehow somewhere had got hold of nursery and folk rhymes to entrance me—all near Beloit College which I attended and in the other direction Madison where I worked for a time in the university's radio station. Other jobs: library assistant and when eyes went a bit bad hospital floor washer, dining room helper etc. . . . Retired now at 63.

As with Lorine Niedecker's poetry, much has been left out, but these few words written to the critic Kenneth Cox in 1966 provide us with the biographical gist. Her *Collected Works* should succeed, at long last, in establishing Niedecker as one of the most important and original poets of this past century and in bringing her work into the mainstream, where it belongs. Jenny Penberthy, a professor at Capilano University in Vancouver and the editor of *Lorine Niedecker: Woman and Poet* (1996) and *Niedecker and the Correspondence with Zukofsky, 1931–1970*

(1993), devoted nearly ten years to this project, sorting through the formidable confusion of drafts, sequences, and chronology that rendered a previous attempt at a complete poems (*From This Condensery*, Jargon, 1985) so unreliable and bewildering as to be next to useless.

Niedecker spent nearly all of her life on Black Hawk Island, three miles from Fort Atkinson, a town in the rich dairy country of south-central Wisconsin with a population of around eight thousand. The state capital, Madison, is thirty-four miles northwest and Milwaukee about sixty miles away, east-northeast. Jonathan Williams, of Jargon Press, visited Niedecker in 1962, a year before her second marriage to Albert Millen and subsequent move to Milwaukee:

> Miss Niedecker, I guess in her fifties by now, lives in a tiny, green house out at Black Hawk Island . . . Right out in back is the sparkling Rock River, on its way to Lake Koshkonong. No phone, almost no neighbors . . . The river is a major fact in her life—lying there sparkling and running, often flooding and worrying the people. It's in the poems. The October day I stopped for lunch I found her reading some of Lawrence's letters, which she compares with Keats's . . . Miss Niedecker lives in terms of the communications from Zukofsky and the few others . . . Besides her writing and her extensive reading, she works at the local hospital for support. She is a frail person, like the poems, but sturdy as they also are.

Williams might have added that Niedecker had no indoor plumbing. Only those who've wintered in this part of the world will fully appreciate that particular hardship. At that point in her life, Niedecker lived near the edge of poverty, although during her growing up she would have known reasonable comfort. Her father, Hank, seined for carp in the lake and rented out a couple of small houses to fishermen:

> He could not
> —like water bugs—
>   stride surface tension
>   He netted
> loneliness

This is from a long poem, or series, titled "Paean to Place," written in 1968. Hank Niedecker, an amiable but loose character, mismanaged his business and when he died in 1954 left his only child some land and the two small houses, which were a nuisance but provided her with a modest income. Of her mother, who became deaf shortly after Lorine's birth and was described by Niedecker's friends as taciturn, embittered, and difficult, the daughter wrote in "Paean to Place":

> I mourn her not hearing canvasbacks
> their blast-off rise
>   from the water
>   Not hearing sora
> rails's sweet
>
> spoon-tapped waterglass-

descending scale-
    tear-drop-tittle
        Did she giggle
as a girl?

Twenty-two years earlier, in her first tiny collection, *New Goose*, Niedecker writes:

The clothesline post is set
yet no totem-carvings distinguish the Niedecker tribe
from the rest; every seventh day they wash:
worship sun; fear rain, their neighbors' eyes;
raise their hands from ground to sky,
and hang or fall by the whiteness of their all.

The elements of Niedecker's mature style are evident here, an amalgam of Mother Goose (viz. the book's title) and what she called "folk poetry," which incorporated certain characteristics of local speech—diction, cadence—along with the terseness and flatness of tone common to the American rural Midwest: Protestant, stoic, of necessity valuing thrift above other virtues. Niedecker doesn't seem to have had any interest in God or religion, at least in its institutional manifestations, but there is, probably unintentionally, something of the Shaker austerity in her work, what Jonathan Williams describes in this poem, circa 1959, as "a lovely sound, put together with hand-tooled pegs":

My friend tree
I sawed you down

but I must attend
an older friend
the sun

Niedecker's work emphasizes proportion, line, simplicity. The spaces between words and lines, usually emphasized in the typography, lineation, and enjambments, functioned for Niedecker as a reminder of the silence from which the poems emerged, by which they were pervaded, and to which they returned. Despite their distinct musical effects, the poems were designed for the page, not to be read aloud. As her letters make clear, she was most decided in this matter.

Nobody, nothing
ever gave me
greater thing

than time
unless light
and silence

which if intense
makes sound . . .

(*"Wintergreen Ridge"*)

Niedecker claimed in a 1966 letter to Kenneth Cox (the punctuation is hers) that

without the Feb. 1931 issue of *Poetry* edited by Louis Zukofsky
I'd never have developed as a poet—I literally went to school

to William Carlos Williams and Louis Zukofsky and have had the good fortune to call the latter friend and mentor. Well— there was an influence (from *transition* and the surrealistes that has always seemed to want to ride right along with the direct, hard, objective kind of writing. The subconscious and the presence of the folk, always there. *New Goose* . . . is based on the folk, and a desire to get down direct speech (Williams influence and here was my mother, daughter of the rhyming, happy grandfather mentioned above, speaking whole chunks of down-to-earth (o very earthy) magic, descendant for sure of Mother Goose (I her daughter, sits and floats, you know).

It is tempting to think of Niedecker as a naïve or primitive artist. This would be a very large mistake. When she arrived in New York City in 1934 to meet Zukofsky, she was already familiar with Ezra Pound's work, along with assorted strands of Modernism, for more than a decade. She was thirty-one and had studied literature at Beloit, a small liberal arts college not far from Fort Atkinson, for two years (1922–1923), worked at the Fort Atkinson public library for two years (1928–1930), and the University of Wisconsin at Madison, one of the best state universities in the country, with enormous resources, was close at hand. She had also married in 1928, although barely two years later she was back living with her parents.

The Objectivist issue of *Poetry* of February 1931 had among its contributors Zukofsky, Carl Rakosi (another Wisconsiner), Charles Reznikoff, Basil Bunting, John Wheelwright, Kenneth Rexroth, Robert McAlmon, George Oppen, William Carlos

Williams, and Whittaker Chambers—a friend of Zukofsky's from Columbia who, among other things, later translated *Bambi* from the German. Quite a diverse lot, although most of them incorporated key elements of the Modern: speed, compression, resistance to closure, obliquity, fragmentation, collage, surprise in transition and juxtaposition, polyvalency, and blocks of description, narrative, or emotion reduced to the telling image or detail. They didn't like Tennyson very much.

Just the mix to excite a brilliant, intellectually restless gal from rural Wisconsin. Niedecker initiated a correspondence with Zukofsky and two years later went to New York to meet him. It may have been her first time any distance from home. Here is George Oppen's wife, Mary, on meeting Niedecker in New York in 1934:

> We invited her to dinner, and after waiting for her until long after dinner time, we ate and were ready for bed when a timid knock at the door announced Lorine. "What happened to you?" we asked.
>
> "I got on the subway, and I didn't know where to get off so I rode to the end of the line and back."
>
> "Why didn't you ask someone?"
>
> "I didn't see anyone to ask."
>
> New York was overwhelming, and she was alone, a tiny, timid, small-town girl. She escaped the city and returned to Wisconsin. Years later we began to see her poems, poems which described her life; she chose a way of hard physical

work, and her poetry emerged from a tiny life. From Wisconsin came perfect small gems of poetry written out of her survival, from the crevices of her life, that seeped out into poems.

Mary Oppen gets Niedecker all wrong. Even indelicate, middle-aged New Jersey boys arrive late for dinner in New York after losing themselves in the subway system. According to Zukofsky's best friend, Jerry Reisman, Niedecker arrived in New York already in love with Zukofsky. Shortly after introducing herself, Niedecker began unpacking and, to Zukofsky's distress, produced an iron and ironing board. She had every intention of staying for a while. Zukofsky lived in a one-room apartment. An affair between the two began. According to Reisman, Zukofsky went to Dr. William Carlos Williams for birth-control instructions, which he somehow got all wrong: Niedecker became pregnant, with twins. Zukofsky was determined that she have an abortion, and she reluctantly acceded. After this, she began an affair with Reisman, and was back in Wisconsin a few months later.

By the time she went to New York, Niedecker had been an energetic surrealist for five years, influenced, as she told Kenneth Cox, by Eugène Jolas's *transition* magazine, already up and running in Paris by 1927, which was devoted to the experimental and what Jolas called the "vertical" in writing. The seventh point in Jolas's statement about poetry, published in the twenty-first issue of *transition*, went: "The transcendental 'I' with its multiple stratifications reaching back millions of years is related to the entire history of mankind, past and present, and is brought to the surface with the hallucinatory irruption of images in the dream, the daydream, the mystic-gnostic trance, and even the psychiatric condition."

Niedecker fell hard for this phantasmagoric geology lesson, precipitating years of experiment with a brand of Surrealism inclining more toward automatic writing and disjunct language formation than dream imagery. Zukofsky tried to wean her away from this, but she remained stubbornly attached to the "subliminal" and managed over time to incorporate inflections of the surreal into her most objective, folksy poems. This may be her most remarkable and singular achievement. The "subliminal" elements are embedded in cadence and sound; there are subtle shifts in movement, alterations of conventional syntax, word-play, and unpredictable rhymes, establishing closure where one doesn't expect it:

> My life is hung up
> in the flood
> a wave-blurred
> portrait
>
> Don't fall in love
> with this face—
> it no longer exists
> in water
> we cannot fish

❁

Club 26

Our talk, our books
riled the shore like bullheads
at the roots of the luscious
large water lily

Then we entered the lily
built white on a red carpet

the circular quiet
cool bar

glass stems to caress
We stayed till the stamens trembled

❁

Remember my little granite pail?
The handle of it was blue.
Think what's got away in my life—
Was enough to carry me thru

Zukofsky and New York were invaluable experiences, but
like a number of brilliant American provincials—Flannery
O'Connor and Eudora Welty come to mind—Niedecker took
what she needed and returned home. She made several further
trips to the city in the mid-1930s to visit Zukofsky and Reisman,
and they made a pilgrimage to Black Hawk Island in 1936, but

Niedecker essentially stayed put in Wisconsin for the rest of her life. Those who argue, groundlessly, I think, that Niedecker and Zukofsky were not lovers cannot deny that he remained the most important person in her life, intellectually and emotionally, over the nearly forty years of their correspondence. The relationship began as an epistolary love affair (at her end, at least) and continued in that vein.

Over time, the Objectivist label came to refer to four poets: Louis Zukofsky, George Oppen, Carl Rakosi, and Charles Reznikoff. Somewhere along the way Niedecker got tacked on to the group, but she was always clear that she didn't consider herself a member. Although Zukofsky admitted that the term never really meant anything, there are unmistakable affinities among the original four. All urban Jews, three of them first generation, they were affected, in different ways, by Pound's Imagist principles, emphasizing exactness, simplicity, sincerity, no superfluous word or sentiment. By sincerity, they meant the honest use of subject matter, without poeticizing or altering it to suit the argument, tone, or shape of the poem. All four were Marxists or Marxist-friendly, socially and politically committed men who came of age during the Great Depression.

Zukofsky was the intellectual of the group. Oppen thought him the most intelligent man of his generation, to whom he "owed everything." Basil Bunting placed Zukofsky, with whom he enjoyed a long, close friendship, as the contemporary, along with Pound, from whom he learned the most. When not offering

Zukofsky birth-control advice, Williams regularly showed him his own poetry before it went into print, without ever really getting what Zukofsky was up to in his work; still, he was drawn to what he called Zukofsky's "word-stuff." This entailed a radicalizing of the Williams line, whose chief characteristic is fragmentation of the pentameter. Zukofsky introduced further fragmentation and disruption of syntax in the service of compression and density. The caesura was also radicalized, creating abrupt stops and extreme transitions. The enjambments became more loaded, incorporating a device from the ancient Greek, *apo koinou*, in which the end word of a line ends one statement, but unpunctuated also starts the next, acting as a pivot on which the next line turns. Prepositions and other particles took on the weight of nouns and verbs—every word, every syllable, contingent on every other. There was a rejection of metaphor. Along with compression and density, Zukofsky wanted to keep the whole thing in motion. Kenneth Cox stresses the importance of Pound's "insistence on brevity of expression" to Zukofsky and Niedecker.

> Grandfather
> advised me:
> Learn a trade
>
> I learned
> to sit at a desk
> and condense

No layoff

from this

condensery

(*"Poet's work"*)

Niedecker always regarded Zukofsky as her mentor, a role he doubtless encouraged. And there should be no question about how much she learned from him and how useful he was in the formation of her mature style and its development. His comments on the poems were invaluable, and though not always taken up, always seriously considered. But it was a two-way street from the very beginning. No one better understood Zukofsky's own difficult poetry, a poetry that usually operated beyond the "edge of meaning," to use Cox's words. And Zukofsky knew it. They freely cannibalized each other's letters throughout the 1940s for their own poetry, and not just the ones each had received from the other. Niedecker, at least, mined her own letters to Zukofsky for useful bits.

Zukofsky married Celia Thaew in 1939 and they had a son, Paul, in 1943. This didn't put a damper on Niedecker and Zukofsky's correspondence; Paul's development became a source of fascination for Niedecker, resulting in an important sequence titled "For Paul and Other Poems," much of it addressed to the child and rooted in things Zukofsky had written to her about his son. It is particularly problematic for any Niedecker editor: there are many versions, she changes the order on several occasions, and so on. The sequence was intended to make up her second collection, but it was never published. Zukofsky, at a certain point, felt his privacy was being invaded and decided to be unhelpful. The collection was dissolved and individual poems published here and there.

The sequence includes one of the finest Zukofsky poems Zukofsky never wrote:

> Paul
>> when the leaves
>>> fall
>
>> from their stems
>>> that lie thick
>>>> on the walk
>
>> in the light
>>> of the full note
>>>> the moon
>
>> playing
>>> to leaves
>>>> when they leave
>
>> the little
>>> thin things
>>>> Paul

My guess is that this poem is directed to the father, a tribute of sorts, as well as to the child. It has all the characteristic sound patterning and delicacy of Zukofsky's finest work.

Another of the poems, not related to Paul but ostensibly autobiographical, illustrates something of Niedecker's range:

In the great snowfall before the bomb
colored yule tree lights
windows, the only glow for contemplation
along this road

I worked the print shop
right down among em
the folk from whom all poetry flows
and dreadfully much else.

I was Blondie
I carried my bundles of hog feeder price lists
down by Larry the Lug,
I'd never get anywhere
because I'd never had suction,
pull, you know, favor, drag,
well-oiled protection.

I heard their rehashed radio barbs—
more barbarous among hirelings
as higher-ups grow more corrupt.
But what vitality! The women hold jobs—
clean house, cook, raise children, bowl
and go to church.

What would they say if they knew
I sit for two months on six lines
of poetry?

As Jenny Penberthy observes in her introduction to *Niedecker and the Correspondence with Zukofsky*: "Looked at as a whole, her work has little of the clean-lined detachment of the core Objectivists. It is shot through with personality, but this is almost always the personality of others. Her own place in the poems remains carefully mediated."

Niedecker's isolation and reading habits played a part in the personae adopted in her work. In a letter to Cid Corman, her friend, champion, literary executor, and chief correspondent in the last decade of her life, Niedecker writes, appreciatively, on receiving a copy of a new Corman book: "You now inhabit a corner of my immortal cupboard with LZ (especially the short poems), Emily Dickinson, Thoreau, Lucretius, Marcus Aurelius, John Muir, bits from Santayana, D. H. Lawrence, Dahlberg, William Carlos Williams, and haiku. These knew 'when / to listen / what falls / glistens now / in the ear.'"

After the deaths of her mother in 1951 and her father in 1954, to both of whom she was uncommonly close, and before her marriage in 1963, she kept to herself. She had a friend or two, at least one serious romance; otherwise she worked, wrote letters and the occasional poem, and read. Her education was through reading and her correspondence with Zukofsky. She never had or hankered after any institutional association:

> Your erudition
> the elegant flower
> of which

my blue chicory

at scrub end

of campus ditch

illuminates

Letters were her social element: there were the letters from Zukofsky and, later, Corman, but her reading, too, consisted primarily of letters and biography, especially the former— Lawrence, Henry and William James, William Morris, Darwin. When Bunting visited her in 1967, she was thrilled and wrote to Jonathan Williams: "Basil Bunting came to see me and it was a high point in my later life. I think in my afterlife I'd like T. E. Lawrence to come. And the Jameses—Henry, Wm. & Alice." In some sense, Bunting appeared in her life as Morris might have, materializing from the bookshelf, visiting for a bit, and then returning to the shelf. The membrane between life and letters was more permeable for her than it is for most of us, and this condition encouraged a plasticity in her own literary persona, a breadth of voice, a large collection of masks, the favorite being timid, little, self-effacing Lorine. "Lorine was shy and unworldly," Jerry Reisman wrote, "but she was lively and talkative when with people she liked. Her sense of humor sparkled in conversation as it does in her poetry and sometimes she was surprisingly uninhibited." But she would certainly have known what she was worth as a writer; anyone writing at that level of sophistication understands very well what she's bringing off.

Niedecker died on New Year's Eve, 1970. She had been un-
well for some months. Basil Bunting was in the area at the time,
visiting family by his first marriage. He had been planning to
make a second visit to Niedecker: "One of the finest American
poets at all, besides being easily the finest female American
poet . . . Lorine Niedecker never fails; whatever she writes is
excellent." A former newspaperman himself, Bunting went to
the two local Madison dailies and beseeched them to run appropriate obituaries. Predictably, they had no idea what he was
going on about. On January 2, 1971, the *Capital Times* ran this:

> FORT ATKINSON—Funeral rites for Mrs. Albert Millen, 67,
> a well-known Wisconsin poet, who died Thursday in a Madi-
> son hospital after a brief illness, will be held here Sunday . . .
> she wrote under her maiden name, Lorine Niedecker, and had
> written a number of books of poetry that were published in-
> ternationally . . . Mrs. Millen had been a contributor of poetry
> to many newspapers in the United States.

Jonathan Williams relates the reaction to this news of one of
Fort Atkinson's prominent citizens: "Hell, I didn't even know
the woman. But I heard she had kind of a negative personality."

BLACKFELL'S SCARLATTI

Basil Bunting

In 1964, Basil Bunting began writing his long poem *Briggflatts* on the train from Wylam to Newcastle, where he was deputy editor of the financial page of the *Newcastle Evening Chronicle*. In June that year, Bunting had written to a friend, "Nothing about myself. I feel I have been dead for ten years now, and my ghost doesnt walk. Dante has nothing to tell me about Hell that I don't know for myself." Bunting's poem was completed in a year. At least a couple of reliable commentators think the original version of the poem was several times longer than the completed version. In its final form, it runs about seven hundred lines. Although he'd published nothing in thirteen years and written no new poems as such, Bunting had been filling notebooks. Wretched as he was at his job, and struggling at the age of sixty-four to support two children and the wife he had brought back with him from Persia as a teenage bride, he'd had a transforming experience. A local eighteen-year-old had phoned Bunting out of the blue and asked him if it would be all right if he showed the older man some of his poems. Bunting told him to come around, and the boy showed up an hour later, "long-haired and fairly ragged, with a fist full of manuscript. He said: 'I heard you were the greatest living poet.'" Bunting got a kick out of the young man, Tom Pickard, and found much in the poetry that excited him. He wrote to Dorothy Pound in June 1965: "Well, I thought, if poetry really has the power to renew itself, I'd better write something for these younger chaps to read . . . I planned a longish poem, about 750 lines, which I finished about a month ago and have just revised and sent off to *Poetry Chicago* today. I believe it is the best thing I've done." In retrospect, it looks more and more as if this long poem written late in his life is not simply the best thing that Bunting had done but among the very best poems anyone had done in the twentieth century.

The Poet as Spy by Keith Alldritt is the first full-length biography of Basil Bunting. It is deeply welcome. The text runs to just over two hundred pages, which is remarkable given the range and concentrated eventfulness of a long life, the life not only of a poet and literary scholar but of a man of action. One needs to go back to Chaucer, Wyatt, Raleigh, or Byron to find anything equivalent, and their lives were not nearly so various. Alldritt's biography is briskly, even hurriedly, written in a kind of literary-journalistic mode that is serviceable and occasionally not quite that. The author has written a biography of Yeats and critical studies of Orwell, Lawrence, and T. S. Eliot. Bunting knew Yeats and Eliot; he may or may not have met Orwell. He truly detested Lawrence, first for locking him out on a window ledge at a party (in Paris, I think) and then for slipping him some hashish baked into a pastry and not warning him. Bunting did, however, greatly admire *Sons and Lovers*.

Alldritt mentions only that Bunting thought Lawrence a "jerk," which, given his novels, whatever their merits, comes as no surprise. He also leaves out a number of other details I vaguely recall from my time as a student of Bunting's and later as a visitor, briefly, to the council house where he lived in Blackfell New Town outside Newcastle. Bunting was a font of stories, many of which Alldritt would have heard during the poet's extended visit to Vancouver in 1970–1971. All his stories were entertaining, the majority of them largely true, many of them embellished, and almost certainly a goodly number fashioned from whole cloth. The inventions and embroiderings were not self-aggrandizing but meant only to amuse. Alldritt exhibits some canniness in his siftings and winnowings.

Bunting always thought of himself first and foremost as a Northumbrian man. His mother's father was a mining engineer and colliery manager from Throckley. Annie Cheesman was a harbor to her son Basil throughout her long life, and not just to him but also to his wives and children. The vicissitudes of his adult life required all of her love and generosity, which would have been in ample supply. Basil's father was a remarkable man. His people were from Derbyshire, which his poet son certainly didn't advertise. Thomas Lowe Bunting took a Gold Medal for his MD thesis. He was later elected to the Royal Society in Edinburgh for his work on the histology of the lymphatic glands of all sorts of creatures. Bunting recalled his father's "tiny surgery with a desk about two feet by eighteen inches long and a microscope." Dr. Bunting had an arrangement not just with the local pet shop, which would call him as soon as some poor creature died, but also, apparently, with traveling circuses and nearby zoos, so he managed to have the glands of lions, tigers, leopards, and monkeys on hand with the rest. Bunting remembered that his house was "sometimes full of lizards that had escaped from their box in the cellar."

But the older Bunting was a good deal more than a distinguished physiologist and physician. He was an early Fabian and took a serious interest in the circumstances of the coal miners who made up a good share of his practice. The politics argued in the household with men like Graham Wallas were decidedly anticapitalist. Basil's parents were also members of Newcastle's Literary and Philosophical Society. As a local journalist many years later, Basil Bunting could be found on wet lunchtimes in the Lit and Phil, where reporters were allowed to use the reading room.

Basil's father read Wordsworth to his son and took the boy climbing in the Lake District. The family was deeply involved in the musical culture of Newcastle, and Basil was a trained chorister who considered a professional career in music. This training was evident years later in the intricate modulations and timbres of his reading voice. But most important, perhaps, Bunting was raised in an atmosphere of Quakerism, though his parents were not members of the Society of Friends. He was educated in Quaker boarding schools and was a conscientious objector during the First World War. He spent periods in the Newcastle Guardroom and Wormwood Scrubs, where he almost certainly took some serious knockings-around. It is a subject he chose thereafter not to discuss.

After prison, Bunting settled for a time in London. He would be away from Northumberland, apart from circumscribed visits, until 1952, when Mossadeq threw him out of Persia (he was then the *Times* correspondent in Tehran and probably an intelligence operative as well). His life during these thirty years makes up the bulk of the Alldritt biography: the principal locales, after London, are Paris, Rapallo, Berlin, America, the Canaries, Persia, Sicily, Tuscany, and back and forth. He drops out of the London School of Economics. He is arrested in Scandinavia while trying to enter Russia so he could put Lenin straight. In Paris he works as a road digger, an artist's model, and Ford Madox Ford's assistant at *The Transatlantic Review*, a job Ezra Pound managed to find him after helping Bunting get out of jail (for drunk and disorderly behavior, that time), a very old jail where Villon had also been incarcerated. Pound found the younger poet with a copy of Villon, a fact that ever after endeared the deeply hungover and trembling young man to his liberator.

Pound was a large force in Bunting's life, as a friend and a teacher. He was fifteen years older and of a different temperament, but the two became very close when Bunting followed him and his wife Dorothy down to Rapallo, and remained close until the late '30s, when Bunting broke with Pound over his fascism and anti-Semitism. It was a private falling-out. Bunting was always to defend Pound, tooth and claw, in public. He remained good friends with Dorothy and took considerable interest in the Pounds' son, Omar. Wordsworth and Whitman were Bunting's earliest masters, but the Pound of "Homage to Sextus Propertius" was the chief influence of his twenties and farther along still. The concentration of sharply observed detail, the flexible rhythms determined by musical phrase instead of fixed meters—all of this was incorporated into Bunting's mature work. From Pound as well he almost certainly picked up the importance of the poet as translator: learning poems in their original language, examining the structures, patterns, methods of expressiveness, and bringing them across in English, or trying to, all in the service of making it new.

During a winter in Rapallo with Pound and his circle in 1930, while browsing in the bookstalls along the harbor quays in Genoa, Bunting came across Kamo no Chōmei's work in prose, the *Hōjōki*, later adapting it into English as a long poem, "Chomei at Toyama," one of his more considerable successes. It was along these same quays that Bunting made the discovery that would most change his life. He came on a French translation of the Persian poet Ferdowsi's epic *Shahnameh* (Book of Kings), a poem of nearly sixty thousand couplets. Pound bought Bunting a three-volume edition of the *Shahnameh* in Farsi, and Bunting taught himself the language so he could get to the poem in the original.

Ten years later, Bunting enlisted to fight in the Second World

War (a "good war" worth fighting), having faked his way through the eye exam and into the RAF with the aid of one of his father's old cronies. After working with balloons in Hull and off the east coast of Scotland, Bunting succeeded in getting himself assigned to what had by then been renamed Iran as a translator and interpreter for an RAF squadron there. He knew only a very antique and literary Farsi, but this was to his benefit when he had to deal with Bakhtiari tribesmen: they understood him just fine, and relations with them were very important in keeping the Germans away from the Anglo-Persian oil refinery at Abadan near the head of the Persian Gulf.

So far as I can make out, there is nothing at all improvisational about Bunting the poet. He is the most deliberate of makers, every vowel, pitch, and duration considered and part of a pattern among other patterns that make up a structure he had in mind before he began the poem. For *Briggflatts* there is even in existence a drawing he made laying out the structure of the poem, and the drawing in turn emulates the sonata structure one encounters in Scarlatti. In fact, he was thinking of Scarlatti's Sonata in B Minor, L.33, at least in the second part of the poem's fourth movement. Scarlatti's sonata L.204 would go between the first and second movements of the poem, L.25 between the second and third, L.275 between the third and fourth, and L.58 between the fourth and fifth movements. The other structural model is the interlaced ornamentation of the Lindisfarne Gospels with their numerous twinings and interrelationships.

Through Pound and Ford, in 1927, Bunting was offered the job of music critic in London for the *Outlook*. He liked to tell the story that he received a call from Otto Theiss, the weekly's literary editor, who asked him if he knew anything about music. Bunting replied, "Not a damn thing!" Theiss told him he'd better learn quickly, then, because he was the new music critic. Learn he did: Bunting was instrumental in introducing Schoenberg to a new English audience. He championed Elizabethan composers like Byrd, then outside the performance canon, as well as Palestrina, Monteverdi, Lully, and Purcell. Along with Pound he helped introduce and popularize the work of Vivaldi, who was known hardly at all.

It was this sort of enterprise and acumen and appetite that he brought to intelligence work. He appears to have been brilliantly suited to it and thrived as never before, discovering in himself facets and strengths he hadn't known existed. He turned out to be an astute judge of men and situations, a more than able commander whom other men would put trust in and follow without hesitation. He was always fearless, recklessly so (except when it came to his American brothers-in-law from his first marriage, who filled him with terror), a man who liked to live by his wits outside the prescriptions of any institution.

He had always been obstinate, rambunctious, impulsive. In dame school and in the family nursery, which was presided over by a Miss Wraith, he brought on himself not a few spankings. Bunting thrived at his first Quaker boarding school, Ackworth, but was sent by his father to Leighton Park School in Berkshire for sixth form so that he might have a better chance at Cambridge or Oxford. It was a rough transition. In 1916, Bunting presented his headmaster at Leighton Park with a document that read, in part: "I have utterly failed to be happy here . . . I think there must be some great underlying difference between North & South which makes people with Northern manners comfortable & easy to deal with, but people with Southern manners are, for me, utterly *impossible* & hateful . . . I think it is your duty to give me my fare to Newcastle . . ." I don't believe Bunting's feelings about "Southrons" (as he called them) ever really changed.

Few men have so enjoyed a war as did Bunting in Persia and the Near East during the Second World War. Among other things, his material circumstances changed. The man who had struggled against terrible poverty (and would struggle again on his return to Britain in the early '50s) lived in considerable comfort, if not opulence. He adored the Persian people, their fatalism, hedonism, dignity. He became deeply knowledgeable not only about their literature but also their other arts and broader culture.

Bunting rose through the ranks swiftly: flying officer, flight lieutenant, squadron leader, retaining that rank until 1954. As early as 1941 he was recommended for a commissioned rank in the Intelligence Branch. It is unclear just how much authority Bunting ultimately had in British Intelligence, although some commentators have him, in effect, as its Near East director. In 1945, as vice-consul in Isfahan, Bunting wrote to Louis Zukofsky:

> my taste for variety has certainly been gratified in this war. I have been on almost every British front worth being on except Dunkirk, travelled through every rank from Aircraftsman First Class to Squadron-Leader . . . , seen huge chunks of the world that I wouldn't otherwise have visited, been sailor, balloon-man, drill instructor, interpreter, truck driver in the desert, intelligence officer of several kinds, operations officer to a busy fighter squadron, recorder of the doings of nomadic tribes, labour manager, and now consul in a more or less crucial post.

On his way home to England in 1946, Bunting again wrote to Zukofsky, this time from a transit camp in Cairo:

> So my responsibility for telling our two governments what happens in Western Asia—between the Jordan and the Indian border, between the Hadhramaut and the Ukraine—is ended at last. So are the pleasant journeys ended, amongst mountain tribes, long trips on horseback, moufflon hunts, banquets with provincial governors and cocktail parties with diplomats . . . All the tribesmen ask the same question: "Why are you taking these officers away from us? Who will be left to understand the Kurds and tell the Powers what we need?"

Bunting also fell dramatically in love in Persia, and of all the tales recounted in Alldritt's book, his marriage to Sima Alladadian, a Kurdo-Armenian from an affluent family in Isfahan, at the British embassy in 1948 is the most beguiling and beguilingly told. Bunting was forty-eight; his bride was fourteen. The Foreign Office was obliged to fire him under these circumstances, and Bunting became a correspondent for the *Times*.

The marriage, Bunting's second, lasted thirty years and produced two children, and I'm sure there must be a few grandchildren knocking about. I met the second Mrs. Bunting in 1978 when I visited Basil at Blackfell. By that time the two had divorced, but Sima regularly looked in on the old man. There remained great affection between them, and Sima liked nothing better than taking the piss out of him, especially in front of an adoring young American admirer. She made us a beautiful Persian dinner of lamb in pomegranate sauce and said, "Do you know why I divorced him? Because he promised me he would die twenty years ago and he never did. The old bastard will never die. He's preserved in whisky and cigarette smoke!" Basil laughed his always alarmingly violent sixty-years-of-unfiltered-Players chain-smoker's laugh. Sima was very much a Near Eastern woman: warm, voluble, emotionally intense, sharp as a tack. Now forty-four years of age, she was an extremely handsome woman with a strong sexual presence. Basil was very proud of her.

Bunting is, I think, preeminent among modern love poets. *Briggflatts* itself, a uniquely dense weave of many motifs, is first and last a love poem to a girl named Peggy Greenbank, whom Basil had met at Briggflatts in 1913 when he was thirteen and Peggy was eight. It was a relationship that continued for six years, with Basil making the

> train journey across the Pennines to spend his holidays with his sweetheart. During one of his later holidays when he was about seventeen and Peggy thirteen, they crept into the old whitewashed meeting house with its heavy mullioned windows and under the wooden gallery inside went through a pretend Quaker marriage ceremony together.

Upon completing *Briggflatts* in 1965, and through the good offices of his younger poet friend Gael Turnbull, he found the white-haired Peggy, now married and the mother of two grown daughters, near Wolverhampton in the West Midlands. Having not seen her in fifty years, Basil turned up with a copy of the poem, which is dedicated to her, and they began a second love affair. Sima, then in her thirties, seems to have been amused, Peggy's husband somewhat less so.

Bunting, like Balthus, a painter he greatly admired, had an aesthetic fascination with the young female form. Not long before Bunting's death, an acquaintance arranged to have him visit the 1938–84 Balthus retrospective at the Centre Pompidou in Paris, an experience he cherished. He seems never to have gotten into trouble over this interest—except when he ran afoul of the British Foreign Office for his relationship with Sima—and quite clearly liked adult women, too. The love poems he wrote in the '20s, in his twenties, are unusually mature, singular, and accomplished. At the time I visited him, he was in his seventy-eighth year and had recently suffered a mild stroke, although he was still very keen. Something like a Schubert string quartet was being broadcast over BBC radio while he was upstairs doing washing one morning when all of a sudden he was at the top of the stairs screaming savagely: "You're playing it too bloody fast!" A couple of rough little Geordie girls, about twelve or so, liked to come by and visit. It seemed innocent enough: the three of us made a little dance together, which pleased Basil.

Alldritt's book is uncommonly frank and inclusive but never goes into much psychological depth, nor is it any way reflective. Its subtitle, "The Life and Wild Times of Basil Bunting," is a bit sophomoric and would better suit a biography of some rocker or other shot by a jealous girlfriend in a motel room. For those who have previously read Peter Makin's extraordinary *Bunting: The Shaping of His Verse*, Alldritt's book may well seem meager, even superficial. But the books are different in kind and, I think, the judgment unfair. Makin's was the second full-length study of Bunting's poetry. It was preceded, by a year, by Sister Victoria Forde's *The Poetry of Basil Bunting* (1991). Forde had corresponded with Bunting from 1970 and visited him. Bunting read a draft of the book and sent her six sheets of corrections: it is a very useful, intelligent book. The Makin book, however, is of another order. It is brilliant, and of a sustained muscular alertness and erudition that makes it exemplary by any standard for criticism. I doubt it will be improved on and it is most regrettably now out of print, not least of all because Oxford University Press was charging fifty pounds for it. Both books contain considerable biographical information, and both had Bunting's attention and help.

For someone so blatantly dismissive of literary criticism, and for someone whose work has been so shockingly neglected, Bunting has been unusually well served by various essayists, interviewers, and bibliographers. He liked to say that there was no excuse for literary criticism after Dante's *De Vulgari Eloquentia*. The contemporary critic he most admired was Kenneth Cox, who wrote two of the finest essays on Bunting. Another astute critic who had something to say about the work was Donald Davie, who titled his history of poetry in Great Britain *Under Briggflatts*. He writes, in that work:

> The deeply ingrained Englishness of *Briggflatts* has to be insisted on, because British insularity has sometimes tried to push Bunting into the margin by representing him as a rootless cosmopolitan. To such insular prejudice, none of Bunting's foreign attachments—not even his devotion to classical Persian poetry . . . —has given so much offence as his fellow feeling with several Americans, particularly the two to whom he dedicated *Loquitur*, Ezra Pound and Louis Zukofsky.

Davie goes on to say, a bit farther along:

> And so Bunting's existence is an embarrassment to the numerous English historians who would have it that modernism in

poetry was a temporary American-inspired distraction from a native tradition which persisted, undeterred though for a time invisible, behind the marches and counter-marches of modernist polemics.

Postscript: Faber & Faber, the publisher of Pound, Eliot, Hughes, Larkin, and Heaney, brought out *The Poems of Basil Bunting*, the first critical edition of the complete poems, in June 2016, on the fiftieth anniversary of his masterpiece, *Briggflatts*.

TWO SAN FRANCISCO

FEUILLETONS

Christmas Day is as quiet as it gets in San Francisco, especially now, before dawn. On almost any other day I'd have already heard the streetcar rattle and squeal as it emerged from the Sunset Tunnel, only about sixty yards away, the first of the day, round about 4:30 or 5:00, making sure the track is clear all the way out to the ocean. And on any ordinary Friday, the garbage trucks, with their hydraulic whine and thumping, would already be at it not far off. But not today.

It has become my custom on Christmas Day, when circumstances allow, to leave America behind and go visit the Orient, by way of Golden Gate Park—enjoy a lunch there, take in a movie, then repair to the sea, where I do not contemplate the year that has just passed by, nor my sins and inadequacies in the course of that year, nor the million bicyclists, nor even the belching satanic mills five thousand miles over the horizon. I don't really think of anything at all, just take in the heaving, coppery waves and sea air, the little snowy plovers hopping about. In how many cities this size on earth can you go out to the ocean late on a beautiful winter's day and enjoy the sunset nearly all by yourself? As I lie in bed planning my day, I can hear the first streetcar of the day out of the tunnel—6:54—and with it the first light.

H. L. Mencken, who complained about much in America, found little to complain about in San Francisco, a town he visited in the 1920s. "What fetched me instantly," he wrote, on his first visit here, "was the subtle but unmistakable sense of escape from the United States." In a subsequent essay, he wrote, "I confess to a great weakness for San Francisco. It is my favorite American town . . . It looks out, not upon Europe, like New York, nor upon the Bible Belt, like Chicago, but upon Asia, the ancient land, and the changeless. There is an Asiatic touch in its daily life." Mencken goes on to say that "the town is rich in loafing places—restaurants, theaters, parks. No one seems to work very hard . . . Puffs of Oriental air come with the fog. There is nothing European about the way life is lived; the color is all Asiatic."

It's getting hungrier and meaner among the homeless these days, not a few of whom live in the park. The poor and undomiciled would have been called something else in Mencken's day—bums, tramps, hoboes—but he makes no mention of them. Now it is impossible not to. I decide to keep to the paved trails. One hundred and fifty years ago, this part of San Francisco was called the Great Sand Bank, nothing here but windswept dunes. There are a couple of police cars parked in Sharon Meadow, out of the ordinary, near the tennis courts when I pass through, before crossing over to the Dahlia Garden, near the big glass Conservatory of Flowers, then past Fuchsia Dell and out by Clarke Gate into the Richmond District.

Clement Street, six blocks north of the park and the heart of the Chinese shopping district in the Inner Richmond, is hopping, Chinese shoppers thronging the sidewalks, every shop open. It looks like downtown Canton on a Saturday, or as I imagine it to be. This augurs well for the Dragon River, my destination on Geary, the next block over, being open. The Chinese began moving into this part of San Francisco when restrictive ordinances were lifted after the Second World War, and with the later influx of Chinese from Hong Kong and the mainland around 1965, the area became markedly Asian in character. Some fifty percent of homeowners in the Richmond District are now Chinese. You want good eats of the Asian variety, this is the part of town to find them.

On the way to the Dragon River, a Hakka Chinese restaurant, I pass a Jack in the Box franchise with a handful of Caucasians sullenly picking at their french fries and burgers or whatever else was available that day on Jack's Value Menu. I can understand why people eat that dreck in Wyoming where there's nothing better to be had, but why here, where there are more marvelous, inexpensive restaurants per block than bars per street in Killarney?

Hell-o, the Dragon River's open, the woks are hot and the noodles are flying. Heaven. If I committed a heinous crime— say I dropped a piano from a helicopter on the head of Chris Christie on his way out of Alfonso's Pizzeria with longtime Trump henchman Roger Stone—and was asked what I wanted for my final meal before facing the electric chair, I would almost certainly say, "Hakka wine-soaked, meat-stuffed bean curd." And ten minutes later, here it is, coming my way.

I don't know when's the last time I had my Hakka bean curd. A long while, to be sure. And it was a long while since I'd been in a movie theater, at least a year. I had a choice between *Invictus* and *An Education*. I don't know about you, but I find Clint the auteur more than a little strenuous going. I had planned my day in advance, so had read up on both movies. As you will probably know, *An Education* is about a bright, very pretty sixteen-year-old girl from Twickenham who is seduced by a significantly older, Jewish con artist. Although I found the subject matter, well, rather inappropriate for Christmas fare, I decided on the latter.

It just so happens that the last movie I went to was also about a young student, played by Penelope Cruz, having an affair with a much older man, her professor, played by Ben Kingsley. I don't recall now if his character was Jewish, as well. Certainly looked it, though, with that big honker. I had a date on that occasion with a woman close in age to myself. She clearly would have preferred seeing another feature that afternoon at the Cineplex and made that known, but I insisted that Ben Kingsley was a great favorite of mine. She muttered and tsk-tsk'd through the entire movie, presumably disgusted at the folly of older men in their pursuit of young women. It was very distracting. I, on the other hand, who have no opinion on the subject, would put the question to my fellow straight male or lesbian pedagogues:

If you had Penelope Cruz in your Boolean algebra or Urdu class, and she plainly fancied you, would you not, quoting a line from a Frank O'Hara poem, be "practically going to sleep with quandariness"?

An Education turned out to be an excellent movie, on balance, I thought. Likewise the sunset out at Ocean Beach, which I just caught after hopping on a Geary bus to the sea: the vast, red molten orb sinking beneath the dark waves. Christmas was now over in Twickenham, and winding down quickly here. It seemed to me more or less safe at this juncture to get on the streetcar and return to America for a cocktail. Mencken, I feel certain, would have expected of me nothing less.

■

The tenant upstairs is imitating a French horn. I can hear him in the hall up near the front room. I've heard worse up there in the twenty-nine years I've lived in this apartment. I thought maybe it was some sort of solfège exercise, but it turns out that he's "singing through his mouthpiece," at least that's what his fiancée, the trombonist, says. "We're getting married," she told me cheerily when I bumped into her on the sidewalk the other day after having been out of town for a few months. I have been listening to the two of them toodle away for years now, usually practicing scales but sometimes playing together one or another of Telemann's *Canonic Sonatas* transposed for trombone and

French horn. Sometimes they disappear for long stretches with this orchestra or that and someone else parks up there, usually a musician of some kind.

Classical musicians, in my limited experience, are eccentric, in the manner certain science or mathematics geeks tend to be, rather quiet and inward, dwelling in a kind of bubble. My theory is that their brains are straining to remember countless scores at any given moment, but this is probably wrong. There is also now living upstairs a lady oboist. She, unlike the trombone and French horn, is very outgoing. "Hello, August," she always says cheerfully, "I'm the oboist upstairs."

She is often outside in the backyard, chatting with the new tenant on the third floor, a tall, serious, bald young man with an Amish kind of beard who has taken over the garden and spends his days there, unencumbered, it appears, by other obligations. "I'm finding a lot of interesting bulbs in the ground," the young bearded gardener told me, rather sheepishly. He ought to be sheepish. Maybe I liked it the way it was, with just the jasmine, two rather tubercular-looking oleanders, and lots of dirt. "You didn't mess with the dead cat shrine behind the palm?" I asked him. I walked him over to the sacred spot. The gardener had dug two trenches, presumably for drainage or irrigation, either side of the sepulcher, but the resting place was undisturbed. "That's him down there," I said. "And that's where I want him, unhouseled, disappointed, unannealed."

Landing this place may be the best stroke of luck to have be-fallen me in this life. It is a rent-controlled apartment in a neighborhood that has become fashionable over time. The landlord would be well pleased if I were run over by a bread truck, as he might then summarily triple the rent. This is why I look both ways very carefully whenever I cross the street. My semi-official backup plan is a trailer park outside Oklahoma City, where I'd spend my days watching *Sopranos* reruns and throwing empty half-pints of Jim Beam out the window at rattlesnakes.

The woman who lived here for ten years before me would have agreed. When she left the place to pursue a "serious" romance, she said to me, rather resentfully, "You know, you'll never leave." She was all about romance. It was romance that got me here, hers and mine. She was a cartoonist, and I was running with one of her workmates from the cartoon shop downtown. She, the workmate, and I came out here for a visit, and the cartoonist was way out of sorts. Seems one of her romances had just been let out of jail and stopped by here to pick up a few things he figured he might need. Since the door was locked and no one was home, he broke a window and climbed in. She inquired if I would like to be her roommate, just in case any other romances should come by unbidden.

And that's how I wound up in the apartment, monitoring the romances, as it were. The penultimate one, before the "serious" one, looked like it would maybe get all of us on the eleven o'clock news. This romance didn't want to leave when she got tired of him after a couple of weeks. He just set up shop in the side room, deciding he liked it here just fine. He wasn't a bad sort, really. Anyway, she took to waving a big steak knife at him.

He waved a .38 at her. Many were the unkind words and dire threats exchanged in the kitchen and hallway when their paths crossed. I can tell you I slept fitfully in those days. Finally, Ms. Romance went off to live with Mr. Right. And there I was, which is where I am.

I was about the same age as the musicians and gardener when I arrived in the Haight in January 1981. My first night here, some poor soul in the park was decapitated and the "perp" stuck a feather in the bleeding stump. That was the headline that caught my attention in the next afternoon's paper. It was a rougher neighborhood in those days. No one could say I've "done a lot" with this place. Assorted lady friends and a wife have certainly tried, but it still has the feel of a kind of "museum of arrested development" about it. Still, it's a sprawling three-bedroom railroad flat with a lovely south-facing view of Sutro Forest and the radio tower atop Twin Peaks, and with an ample backyard facing onto a pedestrian park. There's a lot of green out there, and it's looking as if this coming spring the garden will be quite the spectacle. Actually, it's terrific what the Amish has done, and I'm delighted, so long as he stays clear of the shrine. He's planted all manner of succulent and cactus, flowers and shrubs, vegetables and herbs, ground cover, and put down flagstones, making a little social area where the musicians sometimes gather to sit around shooting the breeze, drinking beer or wine and enjoying a smoke in the afternoon. It's so heartening to me that young people are still drinking and smoking in the afternoon.

When young writers ask me, with that starry, glazed look they get in their eyes, What's the most important thing for a young writer to know or do?, I tell them, without exception (unless their daddy owns Macy's), to try to find a rent-controlled apartment.

Unlike the young aspiring artists and writers today, gathering in places like San Francisco's Mission District and Brooklyn back east, working long hours in hateful jobs to make rent, I was able to pretty much fake it through my thirties, grabbing scut work here and there when necessary. Come to think of it, during that decade I spent an awful lot of time digging up blackberry roots and drinking beer in the backyard. I suppose that's the reason, as the trombonist upstairs goes through her scales this morning, a noise most would probably find intrusive or annoying, I find it to be music to my ears.

CHRISTOPHER MIDDLETON

Christopher Middleton hated New York. Among the things he particularly disliked, I suspect, is New York's position as a cultural bazaar, where reputations are bought, sold, and traded, with the attendant buzz of speculation. He was incapable of schmoozing, and his career suffered accordingly. New York's greatest draw, people action and brute energy, would have been lost on him.

In 2012, Middleton traveled to New York to receive an award from the American Academy of Arts and Letters. He was in his mid-eighties. Recognition of his work in the English-speaking world had been scarce, which is probably why he bothered to make the trip. Perhaps it was always unlikely that someone whose models were Hölderlin, Mallarmé, Tzara, Robert Walser, and Gottfried Benn would win prizes, honors, or even a sizable readership in Britain or the United States. And his poetry has a prickliness about it, as did the poet: a quality of neither asking nor needing to be liked.

In any event, he would have been pleased to return home to Austin, where—after his childhood in Cornwall and degree at Oxford and teaching in Zürich and London—he had been living for the last fifty years. He owned a flash pair of cowboy boots but not a Stetson. Austin and the University of Texas were at their very best when Middleton arrived there in 1961 as a visiting instructor; he settled permanently in 1966, leaving a soon-to-be ex-wife and three children behind in London. Harry Ransom, then president and later chancellor of the university, was determined to make it a cultural center, a not incurious notion. He proposed "that there be established somewhere in Texas—let's say in the capital city—a center of our cultural compass—a research center to be the Bibliothèque Nationale of the only state that started out as an independent nation." Ransom had recruited scholars and writers like Roger Shattuck, Donald Carne-Ross, William Arrowsmith, and others who would have been more likely to land in the Ivy League or the great state universities. So Middleton wasn't wanting for company. The poet David Wevill was a longtime friend and neighbor. The brilliant Swedish poet and fiction writer Lars Gustafsson turned up in 1974 and kept Christopher both amused and busy translating his poetry into English. John Silber, who later became a reactionary megalomaniac (first as president of Boston University and then as failed gubernatorial candidate), was at that point a brilliant and progressive dean of the College of Arts and Sciences, also brought in by Ransom. The music scene—Willie Nelson, Waylon Jennings, and the "outlaw" country set—was about to get going, and the honky-tonks were beginning to jump. The town itself was becoming a magnet for the counterculture. There would have been few better places for someone like Middleton to land. He liked birds, and Austin, it seems, is on a migratory flight path. I'm not sure there's a birdcall Christopher didn't know.

Movement is central to any given Middleton poem. They all have an improvisatory, unstable feel to them and are dancelike, a dance of the intellect, if you will, and in these qualities have an affinity with the painting of Paul Klee. His syntax plays a critical role, with its orderings, the alternating presences and absences, its copulae or want of; clauses gone floating from the main substantive and verb; periodicity, abrupt declarative bursts. The poems have a tense, torqued character. The transitions are unpredictable and the sensibility feels more European than English. They read as if the author had, like Joyce, a variety of other languages going on in his head at any given time:

> But all the time these bats flick at me
> And plop, like foetuses, all over the blotting paper.
> Someone began playing a gong outside, once.
> I liked that, it helped; but in a flash
> Neighbours were pelting him with their slippers and things,
> Bits of coke and old railway timetables.
>
> I have come unstuck in this cellar. Help.
> Pacing up and down in my own shadow
> Has stopped me liking the weight it falls from.
> That lizard looks like being sick again. The owls
> Have built a stinking nest on the Eighteenth Century.
>
> ("Edward Lear in February")

Middleton was also one of the preeminent translators of his era, chiefly from German. As an essayist he had few peers, though Guy Davenport was one of them. Middleton and Davenport met a few years after the war when Davenport was a Rhodes Scholar at Oxford. I hadn't known of the connection until I sent a copy of my first collection of poetry to Davenport, who, along with Middleton, had written a blurb for it. Davenport wrote back something like: "Did you know that when you were in your nappies, young man, Christopher Middleton and I were knocking around Italy together, taking in the cultural highlights?" I know he used the word "nappies" because I remember having to look it up.

In 1977 or so, as a rather despondent young man faced with another long winter in Montreal, working at crap jobs paying barely enough to get by on, with no prospects and nobody much interested in my poetic enterprise, I had decided to bite the bullet and send a few poems to Davenport and Middleton. In essence, I was asking them if I was any good. Because if I wasn't, it was growing ever more apparent to me that I had better get down to finding a proper career—at the post office, selling encyclopedias, something. I wrote to them because I thought—and think still—that they were the smartest fellows out there, as well as the least blinkered, independent of any clique. They both wrote back promptly and with enthusiasm. I couldn't have been happier if I'd just won the lottery and on the same day Hanna Schygulla turned up on my doorstep with a bottle of Liebfraumilch in hand.

I never met Davenport, though we corresponded for many years. He wrote absolutely the best letters, ones that always left me encouraged and exhilarated. I finally did meet Middleton when I was invited to teach a semester at the University of Texas twenty years after that first letter. He had lived for many years in pleasantly rustic circumstances beside a lake in the nearby hill country with his partner, Ann Clark, but now lived by himself in a modern apartment in central Austin, undistinguished except for what was inside: the objets d'art, furniture, and books. This is the way he described it: "Since 1984 I've occupied a two-room apartment in an older neighborhood of Austin; Carolina wrens, cardinals, doves and sparrows, the blue jay, the crow, and the mockingbird enjoy this terrain also. I hear the traffic and through the branches of an immense pecan tree, when they are bare, I can discern a distant downtown silhouette." Close by there was an upmarket steakhouse called Jeffrey's that he liked. The routine was that I drove to his place, where we drank some Rhône wine, then proceeded to Jeffrey's, where we drank some more Rhône wine, dined, then returned to his apartment for some more wine. "Are you all right to drive?" he would always ask at the end of the evening. "You bet," I'd assure him, bravely.

When I arrived at his apartment he'd always greet me, a bit dazed, as if he'd half forgotten our plan to meet. He probably had, because, inevitably, he was deep in a book. It might be the *Goncourt Journals*, or *Timon of Athens*, or the letters of Edward FitzGerald. One time it was an essay on storytelling by Marilynne Robinson, the next a little-known novel by Joan Chase set in rural Ohio and titled *During the Reign of the Queen of Persia*. It was at Christopher's that I first heard the piano pieces of the Catalan composer Federico Mompou. On another occasion he recounted meeting Lawrence Durrell, a hero of his younger days, in Paris, and not being at all let down. Middleton's enthusiasms were more wide-ranging than those of anyone else I've known, and wholly unpredictable. He wasn't big on small talk. He would pour a glass of wine and share his excitement about the book at hand, which would, in turn, lead to related excitements about other books and paintings and music and places and things and people. He would have been a glorious teacher to study under. I learned a great deal from him.

Near the end of my time in Austin, I turned on the car radio and there was Christopher, a guest. He and the host seemed to be friendly; he'd clearly been on the program a number of times. The host asked Christopher to read a poem. Then to my astonishment—so anomalous did it seem against the usual chatter and country music that were staples of the show, and in that furnace blast of a May morning in south-central Texas—Christopher read aloud, first in German, then in his own English translation, Goethe's "Night Thoughts" of 1781:

Stars, you are unfortunate, I pity you,
Beautiful as you are, shining in your glory,
Who guide seafaring men through stress and peril
And have no recompense from gods or mortals,

Love you do not, nor do you know what love is.
Hours that are aeons urgently conducting
Your figures in a dance through the vast heaven,
What journey have you ended in this moment,
Since lingering in the arms of my beloved
I lost all memory of you and midnight.

■

In 2013, his health declining, Christopher moved into a nursing
home in Austin. No one is happy in such places. It goes without
saying that someone as intellectually vigorous, selectively com-
panionable, and independent minded as Christopher would be
unhappier than most. He'd sneak away now and then, once even
getting on a plane to visit one of his daughters. Mostly he just
went down the hill to a friend's antiquarian bookstore or to
Jeffrey's for some Rhône wine. "Got to keep the pecker up,"
he'd say.

We spoke over the phone with some regularity. He'd hold
forth on whatever it was he was reading: J. Henri Fabre on the
song of the cicada, a collection of Zen poems, "Tintern Abbey"
(astonished, as if he'd never read Wordsworth before). Another
time he told me he was reading a volume called *Beckett Remembering, Remembering Beckett*, a gathering of reminis-
cences. "And to think," Christopher said, "that I've been stuck
in a shit hole like this for all these years when I could have been
in Paris!"

I spoke to him one autumn evening in 2014. I was out on the deck at my place in Claremont, taking in the last of the desert light, admiring the gnarled, dusty old sycamore whose leaves had finally begun to turn. Christopher was beside himself with excitement over an essay he'd just come across about Baudelaire's contemporary Théodore de Banville. Baudelaire had described the "lyrical way of feeling" Banville shared with those of "least leisure," who in "marvellous instances" of "lightness" attain paradisiacal "higher regions." "That sounds exactly like something you could have written," I said, thinking of passages of his that describe the way the lyric comes into being and operates. "Yes," he said. "Yes, yes, yes . . ."

When he asked how I was, I used to describe whatever I happened to be looking at: the backyard there in Claremont with its sycamore, behind it the sky going pink against the summits of the San Gabriel Mountains to the north; or the garden here in San Francisco; or the Olympic Range across the Strait of Juan de Fuca when I was in Victoria, along with the smell of the sea; or the magnificently broad Tagus and the azulejo tile work on a visit to Lisbon; or the view across the Hudson to the towers of Manhattan. He'd sigh audibly each time.

He missed his old love, Ann. Even Thom Gunn was enchanted by her. Thom was very rarely, if ever, enchanted by women, and certainly wasn't enchanted by Christopher. (Nor Christopher by him, and they could not have been more disapproving of each other's poetry.) He did find himself a girlfriend at the home, a ninety-one-year-old Belgian jazz pianist who'd lived for many years in New York and whose son, to her outrage, had deposited her at the home in Texas. I told Christopher that I had a Belgian girlfriend, too, which was partly true, at least on her father's side.

"Well, how old is she? She's not also ninety-one, I hope."

"No, no, she's forty-nine," I said.

"That's not young!" Christopher said with extreme disappointment.

"It is for me," I replied. "I'm sixty-three."

"*THAT'S NOT POSSIBLE,*" Christopher gasped.

"It's true," I said. There was a long pause.

"Well, that would have seemed to me most unlikely."

■

"And at last he was free," Christopher said, "finally at peace." He was trembling with feeling and it wasn't easy for him to breathe. He had just read the conclusion of the Walser story "The Walk" to me. He went to fetch his oxygen. We were in his nursing home, an upscale modern brick building, a cross between a hospital and five-story apartment block, described in advertisements as a "professional/residential woody enclave just off the MoPac freeway." It could hardly be more manicured or more creepy.

It was about a year since Christopher's doctors had given him forty-eight hours to live. I had found him sitting facing the door in the middle of an ample living room. The walls were covered with shelves of books and assorted objets d'art that his children had brought from his apartment in town after he fell ill. Everything was arranged exactly as it had been at home. He had Mompou playing. I suspect he didn't want me to find him diminished in any regard and put on a brave show.

"Do you suppose," he asked, "that had I stayed in England it might have turned out differently?" He was speaking of his reputation. "I wouldn't have liked all that family stuff, driving the children around to activities and all that." I told him that I thought that Britain might well have stifled his imagination, that he was right to have done as he did. Whether this is true or not, I couldn't say. It might well have been true. It was clearly what he wanted to hear.

■

Some years ago, after a divorce, I undertook a major cull of my books. I gathered hundreds upon hundreds, lined them up on either side of my hallway, and arranged for a sympathetic bookman to pay me what he thought was fair. "Are you okay?" he asked when he laid eyes on them. It was a reasonable question.

The collection grew back, like kudzu. I remarried. The shelves are heavy with new life. One recently collapsed, depositing its contents around the recumbent body of my astonished but unharmed wife. I see myself as similarly embowered. The books are a comfort to have around me, a psychic insulation. At the same time, I look at them with apprehension. What will become of them? In one of my last conversations with Christopher, he confessed that he had been very anxious about what would become of his library, a formidable one, but that his daughter in Colorado had begun building shelves in her house to accommodate them. It, too, was something he wanted to hear, and it gave him tremendous comfort.

During our final phone call, Christopher admitted he was too weak to pick up a pen. For someone who lives to write poetry, a pen is the last thing to be relinquished, even after the books and the capacity to read them. After all the rallies and reprieves, his months and years of confounding the doctors and cheating death, the time had arrived.

A final collection, *Nobody's Ezekiel*, was published a few weeks before he died at the end of November. The tone throughout is valedictory, as one might expect. The poems haven't the playfulness and torsion of his earlier work, but there are a few beauties, one in particular, "Fragment," which no one but he could have written:

> Even if I'd known what you wanted to hear from me,
> I'd have disappointed you.
>> Only in the night,
> toward a certain pitch
> of loneliness,
>> believe me, the dark sweltered
> a marvel for you.
>> A mockingbird was
> inventing a song, it sang on and on;

not a note in imitation,
the song conjugated trills delicate and furious,
melodies broken beyond repair;
it sang to bring the thunder on
and it sang the more
the louder the storm, thicker fell
sheets and sheets of rain.

That was a night in the back of beyond.
Silence becomes you.

There he is, again
    the little owl,
        calling to you.

LOUIS ZUKOFSKY

Born on the Lower East Side in 1904 to immigrant Russian Jewish parents, Louis Zukofsky spent his entire life in New York City, reading and writing and doing as little else as possible. He was abstemious, a hypochondriac, a chain-smoker; he cared little for food, took almost no exercise, and insisted that the windows of his apartment be shut tight at all times: he was very susceptible to drafts. At thirty-five he married a Jewish pianist and composer called Celia Thaew, whom he had met six years before while supervising a Work Projects Administration program. She had had a copy of William Carlos Williams's *In the American Grain* on the corner of her desk; she'd bought it to have something to read on the long subway ride to and from work. The couple had a son, Paul, in 1943, a musical prodigy and now a well-known violinist and conductor.

Over the course of his long writing life, Zukofsky produced several volumes of lyric poetry, a good deal of it splendidly musical, spare, and challenging. It's hard to determine what any given poem is *about*, however; Zukofsky's work is resistant to that sort of reading, and he held that the meaning was embedded in the sound. Kenneth Rexroth, reviewing *Some Time* in 1956, wrote that the poems were "exercises in absolute clarification, crystal cabinets full of air and angels." Here, in the first half of a poem for the two-year-old Paul, Zukofsky seems to have had Herrick's "To Daffodils" in mind:

> Little wrists,
> Is your content
> My sight or hold,
> Or your small air
> That lights and trysts?
>
> Red alder berry
> Will singly break;
> But you—how slight—do:
> So that even
> A lover exists.

As well as shorter lyrics, Zukofsky wrote an eight-hundred-page poem titled "A." He also wrote book-length studies of Apollinaire and Shakespeare, the latter including Celia's 232-page musical setting of *Pericles*. The first 450 pages or so of the Shakespeare book consist almost exclusively of quotations, from the plays themselves and from the writings of scores of philosophers, physicists, painters, poets, religious figures, you name it, based loosely on Zukofsky's notion that "love is to reason as the eyes are to the mind." There was a teaching anthology in 1948, *A Test of Poetry*, very close in format to Ezra Pound's *ABC of Reading*, which placed poems from different eras side by side and evaluated them by measuring "sight, sound, and intellection." He also wrote critical essays and a book's worth of fiction that is slight and mannered, but playful, charming, and at moments brilliant. With Celia he produced a translation of Catullus in 1961, which "follows the sound, rhythm and syntax of his Latin—tries, as is said, to breathe the 'literal' meaning with him." It fails to do this, but it is nevertheless Zukofsky's greatest achievement and, intermittently, one of the most idiosyncratic and memorable translations in English. Here's a patch:

40

What demented malice, my silly Ravidus,
eggs your pricked conceit into my iambics?
What god not too benign that you invoked would
care dream your parrot's skit of ire and ruckus?
And it wants to purr in the public vulva?
What wish to live it up, be noticed—apt as
air is, squandering in my love's amorous
vice longer than you wished it, marred but poignant.

Catullus's carnality makes a good foil for the severe, involuted, and cerebral quality of much of Zukofsky's own poetry.

Zukofsky, like Charles Olson and Jeremy Prynne, is a *monstre sacré*: his reputation precludes any serious discussion of individual pieces of work. The project is the thing, not a particular piece of writing. How we feel about Zukofsky is affected by how we feel about difficulty, a quality greatly valued by what was once called the avant-garde. Zukofsky is difficult, usually if not always. Another problem in assessing his achievement is that his major work, "A," is an unholy mess, an extraordinarily complex, often brilliant and heroic mess, but a mess.

Not all of "A" is difficult or obscure, however. There's a fair bit of prosaic reportage, even actual newspaper items are reproduced; a large proportion is quotation, another large proportion translation. "A-12," which is longer than the previous eleven sections combined, includes, inexplicably, perhaps sentimentally, seven pages of letters from a dopey family friend written while in the army in 1951. Then there's "A-9," which consists of two canzones, written ten years apart, modeled on Cavalcanti's poem "Donna mi prega." The first canzone, using Cavalcanti's end rhymes, explains Marx's labor theory of value, using phrases from *Das Kapital*. The sounds n and r are distributed throughout "according to the formula for a conic section": "i.e. the ratio of the accelerations of two sounds (r, n) has been made equal to the ratio of the accelerations of the coordinates (x, y) of a particle moving in a circular path with a uniform angular velocity." Zukofsky seemed to enjoy such technical challenges and then solving them. To what end this serves the poetry is not necessarily an impertinent question: the purpose of the difficulty is partly the amusement of the poet. The second canzone, a rewriting of the first canzone using the same distribution of n's and r's and the same Cavalcanti rhyme scheme, gives a Spinozan definition of love, using language from his *Ethics*.

"A-14," as Mark Scroggins puts it in his biography of Zukofsky, *The Poem of a Life*, 'begins with yet another meditation on the space program, then shifts through a dizzying array of Zu-

kofskyan source texts . . . transliterated passages from the
Psalms' Hebrew, bits of a biography of Bach, some smatterings
of Montaigne, and—most strikingly—a run of fifty-seven continuous stanzas distilled from Milton's *Paradise Lost*," which
Zukofsky boiled down from the original twelve books of the
poem. These passages, the "meat" of the poem, are spread out
in six-word stanzas over six pages of "A-14." There are also passages from *Heart of Darkness* and allusions to the May 1963
marches in Birmingham, Alabama, and the September bombing of a Baptist church in which four black children were killed.

Not long after his death in 1978, Zukofsky was taken up by
a group of young writers who referred to themselves as the
L=A=N=G=U=A=G=E poets. The work of this group was
always wrapped in self-justifying, crudely fashioned, poststruc-
turalist commentary, and emphasized indeterminism, resistance to figuration, narrative, subject matter, verbal music,
imagery, or any pleasure that might be associated with poetry,
pleasure that they believed pandered to bourgeois capitalism.
They thought of themselves as Marxists (as Zukofsky had
thought of himself early on) and were intent on challenging the
convention of how a poem is read, by generating reams of unreadable poetry and supplementary text. Their real (and amusing) precursors were not Zukofsky or Gertrude Stein, who
were, in fact, signifying up a storm, no matter how bewilder-
ingly, but the more anarchical Dada poets along with the
Surrealists and their experiments in automatic writing. But no
matter: Zukofsky would do, and since he had been architect and

chief theorist of an earlier movement, the Objectivists, the L=A=N=G=U=A=G=E group pushed hard to position itself as the Objectivists' legitimate and natural heir.

Zukofsky edited a special Objectivist feature for Harriet Munro's *Poetry* magazine in 1931. He had been roped into the project by Ezra Pound and then compelled to come up with some sort of manifesto. He did so, but it was largely irrelevant and silly—"In sincerity shapes appear concomitants of word combinations"—and later disowned by Zukofsky, who regretted the business for the rest of his life. One of the poets included in the *Poetry* gathering, Basil Bunting, a lifelong friend and admirer of Zukofsky who never considered himself an Objectivist or had any interest in the other Objectivists, was so exercised by the theoretical nonsense of his friend's manifesto that he published an "Open Letter" to Zukofsky in a Rapallo weekly newspaper, which is reproduced in the Scroggins biography:

> If I buy a hat I am content that it should fit, be impermeable, of good texture, and of colour and cut not outrageously out of fashion. If I am a hatmaker I seek instruction in a series of limited practical operations ending in the production of a good hat with the least possible waste of effort and expense. I NEVER want a philosophy of hats, a metaphysical idea of Hat in the abstract, nor in any case a great deal of talk about hats.

Carl Rakosi, the one Objectivist poet still alive and lucid at the time of the L=A=N=G=U=A=G=E group's appropriation, protested vigorously, as did an older generation of advocates such as Robert Duncan, whose work was heavily influenced by Zukofsky and who resented what he felt was brazen opportunism and a fundamental misreading of the poetry. There was quite a noisy back-and-forth for a while—great fun really. Scroggins discusses all this in a sketchy, gently scolding (toward Duncan), unsatisfactory way. Regardless, the L=A=N=G=U=A=G=E folks carried the day, and when the Library of America recently published Zukofsky's *Selected Poems*, Charles Bernstein, one of the L=A=N=G=U=A=G=E poets, was chosen as the editor. This means that much of Zukofsky's current reputation is based on a questionable reading of the work.

Modernist critics such as Hugh Kenner, Guy Davenport, and Kenneth Cox were earlier advocates and all wrote with enthusiasm and insight about Zukofsky, all three regarding him as the preeminent American poet born in the twentieth century. Donald Davie, if not quite so enthusiastic, admired Zukofsky's shorter poems, their music and their seventeenth-century echoes, of Charles Sedley especially, but also noted Zukofsky's debt to Williams and Pound, particularly Pound.

Zukofsky didn't discount his enormous debt to Pound, even if he felt he had superseded Pound's achievement. He had begun corresponding with Pound after submitting his "Poem Beginning 'The'" to Pound's new periodical, *The Exile*, in 1927. Zukofsky was twenty-three at the time, Pound forty-one and living in Rapallo. The poem was Zukofsky's first serious experimental or Modernist effort, and Pound liked it straightaway, very much. Two aspects of this longish poem presage Zukofsky's mature style: the highlighting of the definite article in the title, and the way the text consists almost entirely of quotations from other writers.

Pound and Zukofsky's long correspondence was clearly stimulating to both men, with Zukofsky holding to Pound's notion that the poet must "compose in the sequence of the musical phrase, not in the sequence of the metronome," while seeing precision, clarity, and economy of language as principal virtues. He would take the idea of economy to a radical extreme, and it is this, along with the scrambling of syntax and confusion of parts of speech, that makes for most of the difficulty in his work—this attempt to fold the universe into a matchbox, as Kenner somewhere puts it.

Zukofsky's letters to Pound, though argumentative at times, tend to be fawning and do not always make for easy reading, especially at the height of Pound's anti-Semitism. Zukofsky had a strange, rather conflicted relationship with his own Jewishness. The youngest son of an Orthodox father who seldom saw his son between his two jobs and the synagogue, he was not a practicing Jew as an adult, nor was his wife, who was also from an Orthodox background. He never hid his Jewishness, though: it comes up again and again in the work. For Zukofsky, Pound's anti-Semitism was a disagreeable aberration in an otherwise brilliant, generous, and enlightened man, and he tended to shrug it off. His friend Bunting could not. (The two met in 1930 in New York at the urging of Pound and became fast friends.) When in 1938 Zukofsky showed Bunting a letter Pound had sent him, blaming Nazi anti-Semitism on the "buggering vendetta of the shitten Rothschild which has run for 150 years and is now flopping back on Jewry at large," Bunting wrote to Pound, "Every anti-semitism, anti-niggerism, anti-moorism, that I can recall in history was base, had its foundations in the meanest kind of envy and in greed. It makes me sick to see you covering yourself with that filth . . . To spue out anti-semitic bile in a letter to Louis . . . is uncommonly close to what has got to be called the behaviour of the skunk." Pound told Zukofsky there had been a "Lot of hot steam from Bzl." Zukofsky wrote back, more or less apologizing for his friend's outburst. Soon afterward Bunting broke off relations with Pound, not only because of his anti-Semitism but also his embrace of Mussolini.

Scroggins doesn't shrink from this episode, and one catches glimpses throughout the book of mildly unbecoming aspects of Zukofsky's character, as one might of anyone's character over five hundred pages, but these remain only glimpses. And there are egregious omissions in a book that is clotted with detail and the dreariest sorts of coming and going. Among the most inexplicable omissions is any serious treatment of the forty-year-long friendship between Zukofsky and Bunting, most of it in the form of correspondence. Bunting's end of the correspondence, at least a good part of it, is available at the University of Texas, but Scroggins makes paltry use of it.

Zukofsky and Bunting's poetic aims remained very close throughout, and Bunting thought his friend easily the most important poet of his generation and, in the introduction to his own *Collected Poems*, after citing the influences of "poets long dead," writes: "but two living men also taught me much: Ezra Pound and in his sterner, stonier way, Louis Zukofsky. It would not be fitting to collect my poems without mentioning them." Zukofsky would have agreed with Bunting about his own importance and influence: it is unclear whether Bunting had the same influence on him.

More peculiar still is the almost complete absence of Lorine Niedecker in this biography, except in an appendix, which is there to argue against the notion that she had an affair with Zukofsky. The Niedecker side of their correspondence (heavily edited by Niedecker at Zukofsky's insistence) has been published, and it is a remarkable record of thoughts on literature, nature, place, and poetic development, even in its severely altered form. Niedecker's letters also find their way into Zukofsky's work, directly and indirectly, in "A." Their friendship began with Niedecker as acolyte and protégée, but over time she became quite as important to Zukofsky as he was to her. The two almost certainly did have an affair, one that resulted in a pregnancy and an abortion. This is of no great importance, but the literary friendship is of central importance in Zukofsky's life and writings, and in American letters. It's unclear why Scroggins fails to take it seriously and why he finds it necessary to deny so vehemently that the two had an affair. Celia has been dead since 1980.

Nor is the relationship between Celia and Louis Zukofsky examined except in the most superficial detail. One is given almost no sense of her character. In Scroggins's telling, no one in the book, Zukofsky included, seems to have a psychological or an inner life. They were, at the very least, complicated characters. If there is a major theme in Zukofsky's work, it is his domestic life with Celia and Paul. Celia and Louis had a close marriage: Louis, apparently, wouldn't even speak on the telephone without Celia present. It is, in poetry, one of the very few significant collaborative relationships between husband and wife that springs to mind. Celia set much of her husband's poetry to music, these settings appearing with the poetry in book form, and was responsible for the 237-page *L. Z. Masque*, a "five-part score—music, thought, drama, story, poem"—set to Handel's "Harpsichord Pieces," which constitutes one voice, the other four being arrangements of bits and pieces from Louis's various writings. It was composed as a present for Louis, and he decided to make it the final movement of "A." It is no less confounding or strange than the rest of the poem, and wonderful in concept and gesture, however unapproachable or difficult to perform.

Rather than read Scroggins, anyone interested in Zukofsky's life should read the interview with Celia conducted by Carroll Terrell not long after Zukofsky's death, which appears in Terrell's *Louis Zukofsky: Man and Poet*. Celia comes across as very smart, a bit stubborn and droll, like her husband, understated and steadfast, determinedly so as regards her husband's reputation. She is clearly someone out of the ordinary.

Zukofsky would have been next to useless away from his

books and desk, and not easy to live with, especially in later life when the years of neglect seem to have got to him. In "A-12," Zukofsky addresses Celia as "My one reader / Who types me." Of herself and her role in Zukofsky's life, Celia says this in her interview with Terrell:

> I worked closely with Louis, but I always felt that his literary work and his literary friends, those were his, and I'd rather mind my own business, stay out of the picture. I think most people always have the feeling that one, either I knew nothing about it or two, I was Louis's housekeeper. I prefer to go into the kitchen and make the coffee and serve it though I was very aware, very knowledgeable about what he was doing.

Zukofsky and Celia produced a lovely little book in 1970 titled *Autobiography*, sixty-three pages long, consisting, according to Zukofsky, of eighteen (I count fifteen) short lyric poems written between 1931 and 1952, with twenty-two musical settings by Celia and five brief autobiographical prose fragments. There are two epigraphs at the front of the book, the first from Zukofsky's novella *Little*, about a very young violin prodigy, based on Paul: "I too have been charged with obscurity, tho it's a case of listeners wanting to know too much about me, more than the words say." The other reads: "As a poet I have always felt that the work says all there needs to be said of one's life."

Scroggins asserts, not unreasonably, that Zukofsky's reputation rests with "A." Similarly, Pound's reputation rests with *The Cantos*, a nine-hundred-page poem that doesn't cohere or succeed on its own terms, though it is a boundlessly more interesting poem than "A." As Bunting put it in an interview not long before he died, speaking of both poems, their size and composition over forty-five years: "in a changing world the long poem is impossible because the world has changed and you've changed because you have to face that world." What makes Zukofsky and Pound important is their shorter poetry and translations; this is where their influence is vast in Pound's case, smaller but significant in Zukofsky's.

Zukofsky has the nonnative speaker's fascination with the English language. He is interested in words as self-enclosed, individual entities within a poem, objects unto themselves, as he would put it. He has the Talmudic scholar's zeal in running any given word, especially small neutral ones like "a," "the," and "all" (*All* is the title of an earlier edition of Zukofsky's collected shorter poems), through every conceivable permutation: semantic, phonological, morphological, even graphical, and not just the word itself but also its constituent parts, and the entire range of valences possible in the relation to the words and sounds around it. "A" has an index of words at the back, which is curious enough, but originally the index was to contain only the words "a," "an," and "the." Kenneth Cox wrote that "Zukofsky's exploration of language looks like a child's exploration of a new toy: heedless or ignorant of its original function, fascinated by a number of other possibilities, eager to test them."

Cox, perhaps Zukofsky's closest and most appreciative reader, changed his mind about the work near the end of his own life. It was a highly unusual and extreme reversal. "What is lacking is afflatus," Cox wrote of Zukofsky's work, "the breath of life that sends a thrill down the spine and gets engraved in the memory. Assiduous industry and cautious calculation do not replace creative energy, they point up its absence." This is a harsh appraisal, and not in every instance justified, but I find it difficult to argue with finally.

A JOURNAL

Monday, January 12, 2004

Four a.m. I spend far too much of my life awake at this hour. Had I the occasional hypnogogic revelation . . .

The day's first streetcar emerges from the Sunset Tunnel, just thirty yards or so beyond my backyard fence at five a.m. It's come to be a reassuring sound, part whine, part rattle, part growl. The more recent cars are of Italian manufacture and more operatic than the previous models. The streetlamps switch off at six and the sky begins to lighten at seven. But I've already fallen back asleep, deep into another round of raucous, shameful dreams. What sort of creature generates such a strange and disappointing effluent?

It is noon in London. The world's news makes its way back to us here on the West Coast of America, riding a sort of reverse jet stream and settling over us in the course of the day like volcanic ash from a distant eruption: the battles decided, the deals already struck, the deaths of luminaries duly noted.

Rain is headed this way, a "Pacific disturbance." I can feel it, the air heavy, taking the edge off the morning's chill, headed this way from China. You can smell it. The flags atop the empty downtown skyscrapers droop suddenly, then begin to billow to the north. The light slowly changes. It doesn't simply darken, it changes texture, growing denser, taking on a bruised cast.

> The winter rain
> Shows what is before our eyes
> As though from long ago
>
> *(Buson)*

Tuesday, January 13

It was the light and hills here that first captured me. There are clear, windy mornings, usually in spring and fall, cumulus clouds framing the steeples of St. Ignatius, commanding the ridge to the north, that always surprise and exhilarate me. It is a particular kind of light I have not experienced elsewhere. Or in summer, when the fog comes in late afternoons, swiftly moving wisps of cloud, erasing first the base of the radio tower atop Twin Peaks, then gradually the entire tower, as if it never existed in the first place. It is moments like that I rue the fact that I'm a writer and not a painter, like Turner, but with a different palette.

I walk out into these hills, often with my basketball, climbing first Stanyan Street, then Tank Hill, where the city opens suddenly before you, north, south, and east—twenty miles on a clear day, the peak of Mt. Diablo rising in the far distance behind the Bay Bridge. Then down the hidden staircases, nearly always deserted, the trees overhead making a verdant colonnade, to the courts at the foot of the Children's Museum. It, too, is nearly deserted, except for the odd dog walker and occasional vagrant. Am I so dissimilar from a vagrant, except for having my own ball? I have spent many hundreds of hours shooting on this court, with its view of the Bay and Oakland hills beyond. One day the view was mysteriously obliterated and my eyes burned, as it turned out by ash from the terrible Oakland hills fire.

There is nowhere that I am more at my ease than in this place, shooting. If I have a poem that I'm working on, I roll it over and over again in my head, like a child rolling a marble between his fingers, feeling the texture and weight of each syllable. You may think me immodest, but I have done some of my best work up here on Corona Heights, that's what this place is called. You might say this is my *office*. Call me a wastrel, if you like.

One morning I was standing in front of my building waiting for a taxi. I had an appointment, for my music column, to visit a harpsichord maker with a studio in Bayview. It was one of those mornings with the sky behind St. Ignatius doing its marvelous electric thing. The cabdriver turned out to be an older Tibetan man named Gualdon. He had had a long and difficult journey getting here years ago. I often find it difficult to imagine the scale of the ordeals so many endure on their way from one life to another. We immediately became good friends, in only twenty minutes, if you can imagine. He was a trained anthropologist but he preferred driving a cab to most anything else. "Nobody bothers me," he said. "I meet all sorts of interesting people, and not so interesting." Although he had a wife at home who seemed to please him, I think he was reluctant at the end of the day to drop off his cab and drive home. He seemed to like nothing better than driving around the city, picking up passengers and dropping them off. He had passed through many incarnations to arrive at the Diamond of Perfect Wisdom.

The harpsichordist's studio in Bayview was in an enormous cinder-block structure that resembled what I imagined to be a decaying Bulgarian penitentiary of the Stalinist era. It was situated in an industrial area on the fringes of a very modest, largely African American neighborhood where once the youthful O. J. Simpson led a gang that purportedly engaged in all manner of mayhem—before he turned his aggression toward running with a football. "This is O.J.'s old neighborhood," I said to Gualdon. "He used to get up to mischief around here, I've read."

"He didn't kill her," Gualdon said.

"How do you know that?" I asked.

"Because," said Gualdon, "I've had his mother in my taxi more than once. She's a fine old lady and she told me so."

Wednesday, January 14

To think, "'Tis the year's midnight" and in only a couple of weeks the calla lilies will begin poking from the ground and the earliest cherry trees showing their buds, those preliminary spring stirrings that will commence their delicate erotic and poetic claims on my attention, and, as always, somehow manage to confuse the two.

Years ago, when I lived in Montreal, January days were so different from those here in San Francisco that I might as well have been dwelling on another planet. The forbidding cold out of doors pressed one inward, farther and more insistently than one might choose to go. When it became too much for me in those close quarters of my tiny flat, I would make soup. It was almost as if a little timer went off in my head: "Time for soup." This lengthy process and the circumscribed range of tasks involved seemed to soothe me. I had a radio. A fellow with a music show on the CBC, the Canadian national channel, was enamored of Erik Satie's *Gnossiennes* and *Gymnopédies*. These delicate piano compositions with their exotic modes, the unresolved chords and melodies, seemed always to work their spell on me, offering me in those dark months considerable solace and musical sustenance. But also, Satie himself, his eccentricities grown outsize in my youthful and overactive imagination, became something of a role model for me, at least during those trying months, and in a trying time, a not entirely wholesome one.

Thursday, January 15

Perhaps it was during those years in Montreal that I became drawn to the radio. I can barely tolerate television, much less sitting in a movie theater. Though I am happy to sit in the dark in my front room and stick a movie into the VCR. I'm not sure why this is. Of late I've been immersed in the noir films of Jean-Pierre Melville, especially if Lino Ventura is on hand. Alain Delon is too pretty. Lino is a hard man, you can tell by the way he carries himself. Melville likes the shadows under train trestles and the violent *clackety-clack* of the trains passing overhead. It's all very neoexpressionist and obvious. But I fall for it every time . . . that is, until I get over it. Then I can't take any more of it, ever. I seem to be that way with any number of my fascinations. Except for the radio. I am endlessly devoted to my radio.

There are some unusual, or out of the ordinary, characters one comes across, sometimes, up at the basketball court. One is a man, perhaps a few years older than myself, who likes to do his tai chi exercise routine up there, "swimming in the air." The legend goes that a certain Zhang San-Feng was awakened one morning by scuffling sounds outside his window. When he looked out to see what the commotion was, he observed a crane and a snake engaged in "mortal combat." From their thrusts and parries he came up with the principle of tai chi, it is said, the balanced alternation of strength and yielding.

We never speak, this tai chi fellow and me. He swims; I shoot.

On one occasion, after not having crossed paths up there for a number of years, we found ourselves there together again one day, doing what we customarily did. We nodded politely to one another and smiled, noting to ourselves, ruefully, the effects of time that had befallen the other, and then returned to our solitary activities.

Then there's the *strange ranger*. San Francisco is long on this type. He's been up there as long as Tai Chi and I. He sits under a shade tree with his boom box. He's aggressively amiable and talkative, trapped in a kind of panic of friendly chatter. One tries to be polite, but you'll be wanting to give this one a wide berth. If he's drinking beer, as is often the case, his bonhomie and volubility expand to a worrying intensity. He'd probably try to kill me, if he could, with his conviviality. He always recognizes me straightaway, having seen me up there so many times over the years, and gets terribly excited when he spots me. I give him my best Duchess of Windsor smile and keep shooting. I think I don't need to tell you what he's always listening to on his boom box, do I? Maybe you've already guessed: Black Sabbath.

Friday, January 16

We don't often get the better foghorn music in this part of town, at least this time of year. In the summer it's not uncommon, but it's rare in January. So when it's blowing full on, as it is this morning, it's a treat. Foghorns, however clichéd you may find the notion, are one of the principal reasons I live here in San Francisco and not Cincinnati.

Which reminds me of a particularly San Francisco morning not so very long ago, a late spring Sunday morning, to be exact, when I awoke in a part of town where I had never awakened before, in the northwestern corner of the city, out near Lands End, close to the mouth of the Bay.

It was dreadfully early in the day to be walking out into that fog and wind, especially fierce so close to the water. You won't find any tourists up at that hour or in this part of town. That morning it sounded like every foghorn in the arsenal was hard at it, trading their booming warning tones as if engaged in some kind of contest.

I made my way, shivering, to catch a bus in the direction of my own neighborhood. A crowd of Chinese people waited at the bus stop, young and old. I might as well have been on a corner in Nanjing, except for the English-language shop signs and the big Russian Orthodox church with its gold onion dome.

Considering that it was Sunday morning and they were all headed off for a long, tedious day of work, the busful of passengers seemed in excellent cheer, chattering away to one another, listening to their Walkmans, heads bobbing to the music. They were clearly made of sterner stuff than I, at least on that particular morning.

I got off the Geary bus at Masonic and proceeded downhill toward the Panhandle. Even before I made it to Fulton, I registered the helicopters overhead and heard the cheering crowds. I was east of the fog now and into the sunshine of what was becoming a very warm day. I had on the previous evening's sports jacket, dress slacks, and oxford shoes.

Presently, I saw, passing before me in an endless stream, thousands, no, tens of thousands of runners, shoulder to shoulder, densely packed, headed in the direction of Golden Gate Park and, finally, the finish line at the ocean, another three and a half miles farther along. Many of the runners were in various stages of undress, not a few buck naked, some in nuns' habits, several inside a centipede costume, one in only a top hat and jockstrap—a female, mind you. There was a cluster of Vikings in loincloths, scores of transvestites, naked werewolves, bishops and babydolls, bishops in babydolls, fatsos in motorcycle caps and leather lingerie, a woman in a cocktail dress with a Laura Bush mask . . . At the front of the pack, already miles ahead, closing on the finish line, were the swift, slender, long-legged Kenyans, perhaps with an Ethiopian or two in the mix, as always, fighting it out among themselves for first place.

I'm not sure what kind of prize money they got for finishing first. It couldn't have been too terribly much, and it does seem an awfully long way to have come, no?

RICHARD BRAUTIGAN

Bolinas is a sleepy little seaside community about an hour's drive north of San Francisco, at the end of a long, winding road over the hills. It isn't easy to find the turnoff, and over time residents have put up misleading signs or camouflaged helpful ones in order to discourage tourists. For many years, a fair number of artists and writers have made Bolinas their home, or one of their homes. One of them was Richard Brautigan. When I gave a reading sixteen years ago at the Bolinas Public Library, a couple of Brautigan's old friends from his North Beach days in the 1960s told me that he had recently turned up in town. I remember hoping that he might come to the reading if he had nothing better to do. But there was little chance of that. Brautigan was lying dead in his Bolinas house, having taken a .44 caliber handgun and shot himself in the head. His body lay there for weeks until finally discovered by friends.

It seems odd now to recall the excitement that attended the publication of his novels, stories, and poems in the late 1960s. Like a new Bob Dylan album, each book was an event: *Trout Fishing in America* sold over two million copies. There was in the writing something that felt new and fresh, of the moment. Brautigan had a lightness of touch, gorgeous timing, and a delicious offhandedness that always managed to hit all the right notes, in just the right sequence—color, pitch, you name it. Breathtaking stuff.

Time has not been kind to the writings of Richard Brautigan. By the early 1970s, the critics were already having a go at him, and with a certain appetite. They were, on the whole, quite right: he wasn't really very good after all. The work is not without charm or felicities of style, but it is pretty thin stuff: precious, self-indulgent fluff. It is also true, however, that had Brautigan been an Easterner, an Ivy League graduate, a habitué of upper Manhattan literary soirées, he might well have been allowed a gentler landing. But he was not any of those things: he was a Westerner, white trash, didn't go to college, and worst of all, was a California phenom, a national success, the literary darling of the young. The long knives were well overdue in making an appearance.

Brautigan came from the Pacific Northwest, born in Tacoma, Washington, in the winter of 1935. His childhood seems to have been appalling and he was reluctant to discuss it. He never knew his father, who, in turn, never knew of his son until reading his death notice. His mother was no bargain either, at one point abandoning Brautigan and his younger sister, then age nine and four, respectively, in a hotel room in Great Falls, Montana. Brautigan grew up poor in Eugene and the small towns of Oregon. In 1955, he threw a rock through a police station window, was arrested, diagnosed as paranoid schizophrenic, and committed to Oregon State Hospital for three months. There are differing stories as to why he tossed that rock. One has it that

Brautigan showed a piece of his writing to a girl he had a crush on and she didn't think much of it, so he got upset. He told his daughter, many years later, that he was simply hungry and figured that in jail he would at least get three square meals. In any event, he miscalculated. He was given electroconvulsive therapy, and his sister, with whom Brautigan did seem to have a tolerable relationship, is quoted as saying that her brother was very quiet when he returned home and never really opened up to her again. Brautigan left for California several days later and he never came back. "I guess he hated us," his mother said. "I haven't the slightest idea why."

The San Francisco Brautigan settled into in 1955 would have been, as it continues to be, a very lovely, provincial port city, with a long history of hospitality toward unconventional outsiders, not least artists and writers. It would, of course, have been a sleepier place then and with manageable rents. San Francisco likes to think of itself as a far-flung version of fifteenth-century Florence, a cultural oasis in a savage wilderness, but, in truth, it has never been a significant center for the arts in America, not in 1955, not now. Perhaps this is because it is such a forgiving place, or was once, and such a remarkably pleasant place to be. Some of the presiding literary spirits when Brautigan arrived in town would have been Kenneth Rexroth, Robert Duncan, and Jack Spicer (to whom *Trout Fishing in America* is dedicated). Writers such as Ginsberg, Kerouac, Corso, Snyder, Creeley would also have been moving through at this point, but the so-called Beat Scene was not fully fledged, and its principals not yet aware that they were beatniks, merely a few young writers on the move, figuring it out as they went along. There would have been a handful of interesting painters floating around, and the jazz in the local clubs would have been thoroughly wonderful and cheap to go hear.

A mutual friend describes Brautigan, circa 1970, as a "funny, terrified man." His reticence kept him from being among the regulars who would get up and read their work at the North Beach coffee bars. His offbeat, gentle humor did not, in any case, endear him to audiences, whose tastes were for the more apocalyptic and expansive. The other Beat writers appear to have found him rather "queer." He was certainly never taken up either by them or the national press as part of the inner Beat circle.

Brautigan began as a poet. "I wrote poetry for seven years," he said,

> to learn how to write a sentence because I really wanted to write novels and I figured that I couldn't write a novel until I learned how to write a sentence . . .
>
> One day when I was twenty-five years old, I looked down and realized that I could write a sentence . . . wrote my first novel *Trout Fishing in America* and followed it with three other novels.

Brautigan began publishing his poetry in assorted magazines as early as 1956. His first small collection of poems, *Lay the*

Marble Tea, was published in 1959. (Marmoreal imagery will occur throughout his poetry and fiction, curiously embedded in similes.) By the mid-1960s, while involved with the Diggers and hippies in the Haight, he could often be found giving copies of his poems away on the streets—probably to pretty young women, if we are to judge by the subject matter of the poems and stories. Brautigan published two full collections of poetry in his life: the first, *The Pill Versus the Springhill Mine Disaster*, appeared in 1968, the same year as his third novel, *In Watermelon Sugar.* That same year *Please Plant This Book* also came out: eight seed packets, each containing seeds and with poems printed on the sides. A second collection, *Rommel Drives on Deep into Egypt*, was published in 1970, the year he was divorced from Virginia Adler, whom he'd married ten years earlier in Reno.

The poetry is just flat awful, no two ways about it, and now embarrassing to read, not least, I suppose, because I was so infatuated with it thirty years ago. Like his fiction, the poems are minimalist, sometimes only a line in length. They rely almost entirely on Brautigan's light touch, gentle irony, and, his favorite trope, the mildly surreal, occasionally startling metaphor or simile. He was too fond of this device, and it sinks the poetry a good deal faster than the prose, which customarily has a bit of narrative shape and movement to keep it put-putting along, if barely. The poetry is hopelessly sentimental, sophomoric; what once seemed dashingly offhand and hip now cloys.

Trout Fishing in America was written in the summer of 1961 in Idaho's Stanley Basin, wild country. Brautigan spent that summer camping with his wife and one-year-old daughter, Ianthe, and the book was written on a portable typewriter alongside a trout stream. It is arguably Brautigan's best book, and although largely rough going forty years later, the writing remains highly original and inventive. Brautigan liked fishing and knew a great deal about it. Many of his stories—his best ones—are about going fishing as a boy, just heading off into the woods and rain with his rod and reel.

Brautigan's prose writings are occasionally grouped with those of certain of his contemporaries—Barth, Coover, Vonnegut, Barthelme—under the rubric New Fiction. There is in Brautigan, as with the others, what Borges called "that element of irrealism indispensable to art"; as with the others, too, a foregrounding of form and language, blurred distinctions between the real and imaginary, time now and time then. John Barth has written about Barthelme's "nonlinear narration, sportive form and cohabitation of radical fantasy with quotidian detail." Along with those traits, Brautigan shares with Barthelme his extreme minimalism, the deft placement, or misplacement, of emphasis, the shaggy-dog endings. But the similarities end there. The color, texture, and tone of their work is completely different, as is the subject matter and its treatment. Brautigan is the looser writer, more radical in form and farther out in his imaginative flights, but he is also less capable of achieving a successfully sustained narrative, no matter how brief. Brautigan is continually bailing out in his stories before they arrive anywhere. Or he is trying to charm his way out. It shows up badly now.

It took six years for *Trout Fishing in America* to be accepted by a publisher, and it was a small San Francisco house, Four Seasons Foundation. *A Confederate General from Big Sur*, a novel written later but published earlier (in 1964 by Grove Press in New York), bombed. Brautigan lived very modestly with his wife and daughter until the huge success of *Trout Fishing*. For someone as gentle, bewildered, alcoholic, and vulnerable as he was, it must have been powerfully upsetting to be taken up so fast, then dropped so hard.

In addition to his eight novels, Brautigan wrote *An Unfortunate Woman*, a collection of diary entries from 1982 that revolve around the death of a close woman friend. It was unkind of the publishers to release the book. Brautigan was by then exhausted and in despair. Two years later he would be found dead with a whiskey bottle by his side and a bullet in his head. The writing is artless, even as a set of notebook entries. Only some of the tired old mannerisms identify the author, but these, too, have grown faint.

Revenge of the Lawn is a collection of short fiction written between 1962 and 1970, sixty-two pieces over 160 pages. The longest of them run to five pages; several are only half a page or less. A few are mildly charming. Brautigan is puppyish and sometimes endearing when he effuses over a new girlfriend: he was a famous enthusiast. More than a few of the stories have memorable or beautifully handled moments of observation. It's a pity he was such a lazy writer. The best story in the collection is atypical. It's called "A Short History of Oregon" and is about coming upon a house in the middle of the Oregon woods:

> As I got closer to the house, the front door slammed open and a kid ran out onto a crude makeshift porch. He didn't have any shoes or a coat on. He was about nine years old and his blond hair was disheveled as if the wind were blowing all the time in his hair.
>
> He looked older than nine and was immediately joined by three sisters who were three, five and seven. The sisters weren't wearing any shoes either and they didn't have any coats on. The sisters looked older than they were.
>
> The quiet spell of the twilight broke suddenly and it started raining again, but the kids didn't go into the house. They just stood there on the porch, getting all wet and looking at me . . .
>
> The kids didn't say a word as I walked by. The sisters' hair was unruly like dwarf witches'. I didn't see their folks. There was no light on in the house . . .
>
> I didn't say a word in my passing. The kids were soaking wet now. They huddled together in silence on the porch. I had no reason to believe that there was anything more to life than this.

Which is how the story ends. Brautigan doesn't get more straightforward than this, nor does he elsewhere manage to be emotionally connected to his material in this way. The tropes involving the children's hair are in harness to the rest of the story and don't jump out or take precedence, as is usually the case. We don't need to know a great deal about Brautigan's personal history to twig that this scene cuts close to the bone.

If we want to know more about Brautigan, the man and father, we could skim through Ianthe's memoir of her father and, gulp, her "coming to terms with his death." *You Can't Catch Death* isn't much of a book but is surprisingly touching in its portrait of Brautigan. He appears as a sweet, loving father, however absentee or alcoholic. If she didn't see a great deal of him over the years, whatever she got seems to have been wonderfully distilled. There is a strong whiff here of writing workshops and California cough-it-all-up therapy. She runs out of material about halfway through and begins writing short chapters in her father's faux-naïve voice that feel like cruel pastiche or parody.

Sometimes, rereading a flawed, or even failed, writer is as interesting as reading the works of "successful" ones, like Philip Roth, say, or Martin Amis, who are strong, sure, and able. With Brautigan, one sees the fissures, the slapdash detail, the failures of nerve and, of course, the steep decline just at the point when it should all have been going the other way. Brautigan was damaged goods, psychologically, from the get-go. It was going to end badly—even his daughter could sense that early in her life. But he is an American original, as much in the trajectory of his career and tailspin as in his writings. It is pleasant to think of the lanky, blond teenager sitting in small Oregon libraries after the war, with the rain pouring down outside, going through the works of Hemingway and Twain, Hammett and Zane Grey, the Brothers Grimm, the poems of John Keats (to make an educated guess). He was also a great fan of Caroline Gordon, all of whose novels he hungrily read, and was perplexed throughout his life that not everyone else had done so. "The pure products of America go crazy," William Carlos Williams wrote. Sometimes, they are simply overwhelmed.

LUNCHING WITH GINSBERG

It would have been February 5, William Burroughs's birthday. Ginsberg was in a panic about having forgotten it (Burroughs's seventy-fifth)—only one among his several panics that gray, frigid Sunday afternoon on East 12th Street. Ginsberg's anxiety resembled that of a favored child loath to disappoint a loving parent. No, that wouldn't be quite it: Burroughs as a loving parent, no. Perhaps it was more Auntie Allen not wanting to let down his weird elderly nephew. There was a fair bit of the doting auntie in Allen Ginsberg.

It must have been 1989, which would have made Allen sixty-two years old. Inside another eight or nine years he'd be dead, but he was looking reasonably good that particular day for an old beatnik. His liver got him in the end—an earlier bout with hepatitis developed into cancer. So the doctors surmised. He wasn't a drinker, and I don't expect he was doing drugs at that stage. He didn't offer me a joint or a line of blow, at any rate. Besides, it was early in the day for any of that.

I was absorbed in taking in the apartment and the measure of the man. I'll let Barry Miles (*Ginsberg: A Biography*) describe the setup:

> In March 1975, Allen and Peter Orlovsky moved into a much
> larger apartment, at 437 East Twelfth Street between First Av-

enue and Avenue A. It had six rooms, two of which were very small, and had been created by knocking together two small apartments: an arrangement that led, somewhat incongruously, to Allen's having a sink right next to his desk in his office. There were three south-facing front rooms . . . with a third becoming Allen's office. When Allen woke in the morning all he could see from the window was the top of the church opposite, which, in the gray winter light, reminded him of his days in Paris . . . They painted the walls white, tacked their picture of the young Rimbaud on the wall, and were home.

More presently about Peter Orlovsky, who was no longer Allen's roommate at the time of my visit.

I remember immediately liking Allen, somewhat to my surprise. He was nothing at all like his cartoonish public persona. In fact, he reminded me of no one so much as my old pediatrician and family friend, Sam Prince. The two didn't resemble each other physically, nor was there anything particular in the manner. I suppose he was just very familiar to me: Jewish, north Jersey; both of us provincials out of a very particular psychosocial milieu; ten miles and twenty-three years apart, growing up in the same light, the same benzene fumes. The same oil refinery fire-eaters flaming the night along the Jersey Turnpike. The same speech patterns, body language, and the rest. I was immediately comfortable around him. I could read him easily.

I suspect he felt the same. There was no pretense or awkwardness. There was no side to him, at least that I could see. There was nothing either of us could do for or to the other. We quickly relaxed into an afternoon's acquaintance. What struck me first, I remember, was his seriousness and intelligence. Poets, no matter how bright, tend to be silly, loose characters, self-involved and oblivious of the world around them. Somewhat like academics, in this last regard—which, in America, almost all poets are, thereby compounding the dilemma. Allen taught a couple of courses at Brooklyn College during those years, but he certainly wasn't recognizable as your conventional poet-academic. He was far too present and sharp, of the world. More like a businessman, really. Not the car salesman or insurance adjuster sort; more the investment banker type, I'd suggest. Or a physician. Which, I suppose, is why he reminded me of Dr. Prince. I doubt one thing has to do with another, but as poets we were both children of another New Jersey physician: William Carlos Williams.

Allen looked the lumpy old boho, but he was astute in that business or physician way, gracious in manner but tirelessly appraising, inquisitive. I found it flattering: that is, to be appraised by someone of that stature and not to be dismissed out of hand as a bore, a poseur, or an outright fool. Ginsberg was, in reality, the CEO of a considerable and enduring international enterprise: Allen Ginsberg, Inc. He had traveled the world, for the most part as a celebrity, and met all manner of people: Ezra Pound, Bob Dylan, lepers, you name it.

It was curiosity, not admiration, that brought me to look up Ginsberg. He had been a huge influence when I was in my late teens, as had been his friends: Kerouac, Corso, Snyder, Whalen,

Burroughs, even poor Carl Solomon, whom Ginsberg had met during a brief incarceration in the madhouse. Collectively, this group was a marvelous tonic (at least to a seventeen-year-old) for the Lowell and New Critical miasma of the period, with its self-conscious, elevated tone; its allusions, ironies, formalist tricks; its insistence on being taken seriously. The self-satisfied, conspicuously elegant poet Anthony Hecht, who was much admired in academic circles and the recipient of a Pulitzer Prize, visited our high school in 1966—on what was called Careers Day, a day put aside for distinguished alumni to speak to men in the senior classes about their vocations. I was quite definite about wanting to be a poet by the time I was sixteen or so. Mr. Hecht, with his vaguely English elocution (acquired in the Bronx?) was definitely not what I had in mind.

I now think more of Ginsberg's achievement, at least early in his career, than I did back then, when I was probably at the tail end of my disillusionment with the entire Beat enterprise. Also, I was contemptuous of the way Ginsberg had shamelessly merchandised himself and "the Beats" over the years, squandering his own gifts in the process. I was contemptuous of his opportunistic hippie Buddhism, his addiction to celebrity and celebrities, the infantile politics (which now strike me as more visionary than infantile), his association with the silly and occasionally sleazy Naropa Institute in Colorado and its Jack Kerouac School of Disembodied Poetics. I was contemptuous of the whole business of being Allen Ginsberg.

Of course, I'm older now and, inevitably, less judgmental. I have also observed, over time, how more *dignified, serious-minded* poets have cultivated their reputations via the critical-academic establishment route—those tireless, decades-long campaigns for Pulitzers, even the Nobel, with all the bartering, double crosses, and leveraging that entails. Of course, this takes place behind the veneer of priestly devotion to the Art of Poesia, the life of the spirit and all that.

Ginsberg, at least, made no pretense about it. He was, figuratively, on the busiest street corner in town, jealous of his position there, and with his skirt up over his head, wiggling his hairy old ass for whatever it was worth.

But the private man was nothing like that, at least that particular afternoon. Sure, he could be self-absorbed, occasionally frantic, wheeling and dealing over the phone in an obnoxious humiliating fashion. But for the most part, I encountered a kind, thoughtful, soft-spoken man: a mensch. The frenzy, the self-aggrandizement, and all the rest seemed a long destructive war that had laid waste his poetry and, probably, any chance of emotional equilibrium or peace.

■

"Are you queer?" Allen asked pointedly, directly after we had been seated in a large, noisy Ukrainian restaurant around the corner. "No," I said, mildly taken aback, but certainly not mortified or feeling jumped. He famously was—and by all reports, at the age of thirty-nine I would not have been his type. He looked at me in his appraising way, not disbelieving me, I think, but probably gauging my reaction. "Just curious," he said matter-of-factly, and took a camera out of his satchel. He began photographing me, right there in the booth. "I hope you don't mind," he said. "I like to photograph people." I did mind, in fact. I dislike being photographed, particularly in a public place by a famous person. But he was mad for photographing and seemed to do it compulsively. He meant nothing by it, really. He'd had shows of his photography, books and so on. It's not very interesting.

We enjoyed a pleasant, starchy lunch: the kasha and farfel, blintzes, kreplach, and the rest. Old World Jew food, leaden, bland, with chicken fat (schmaltz) as a base, in lieu of butter or olive oil. A poor substitute, a substitute of the poor. But familiar to us both from our growing up. A cuisine like the British: dismal, unhealthy, somehow comforting.

On the way out of the restaurant, we encountered the most remarkable woman I had ever seen. At least six feet tall, very black, drop-dead gorgeous, with an Apache's cheekbones and a flattop hairdo—for all the world, like a savage Diana. She also looked very familiar, and she was also looking very long and hard at Allen, eyes narrowed in a not entirely friendly way. And he at her, very intently. This engagement of fierce stares continued for an uncomfortably long time, then suddenly disengaged, and off they went their separate ways, not quite satisfied. What had transpired was two celebrities, encountering one another at short range, recognizing each other as celebrities but not knowing quite who the other was. Allen's celebrity has endured longer than Grace Jones's, but I have never seen such a dramatic-looking creature before or since. I can't imagine what I would do if I was sitting next to someone like that at a bar and she said, "Let's go to my place and fuck." Timidly follow, I suppose, or run off whimpering into the night.

■

Allen invited me back to his place for tea. It was a bitter-cold afternoon, raw in the particular way New York gets in late January, early February. There are colder towns, and I've lived in a few, but cold doesn't get much meaner than it does in Manhattan, with that river wind blowing up the streets and swirling among the buildings. Besides, I was enjoying Allen's company.

There had been that moment when, leaving his apartment to go to lunch, he said, "Wait a minute. Let me just tell Peter I'm going to be gone for an hour or so." This was Peter Orlovsky, Allen's longtime companion, whom Allen had set up in an apartment next door to his. Allen knocked on the door, and no one answered for a long time. Allen kept saying, "Peter, Peter, it's me, Allen." Finally, after five or ten minutes of this, I heard shuffling, the unfastening of locks, and the door opened, at least as far as the chain allowed. Allen explained to a wild-eyed old man that he would be going to lunch with his friend August, and would return before too long. Orlovsky looked at me, looked at Allen, looked back at me, made an unfriendly animal sound, and, teeth bared, lurched forward, face-first, through the space in the door, gargling and shrieking like an enraged beast.

Allen made gently disapproving and comforting noises all the while before, finally, closing the door on Peter. I'm not sure, but maybe Ginsberg had keys that worked from the outside that kept that lunatic in his cage. "Peter's a bit upset, it seems," Allen said sheepishly.

The two men were no longer lovers, but they remained close, literally. Orlovsky had always been mad as a hatter. His entire family was mentally ill. My sister used to meet with Peter's brother Julius, when, as a psychiatric social worker, she was employed in the outpatient clinic at Bellevue. Peter would sometimes show up as well. Now Peter's dementia had been aggravated by alcoholism and, apparently, someone was getting cocaine to him now and again. Which wouldn't have helped. When they first moved to 12th Street, Allen, Peter, and Peter's girlfriend Denise all shared an apartment. This arrangement had altered over time. I cannot imagine the Orlovsky I met in 1989 cohabiting with a woman, Denise or anybody else. But allegedly he did, at least now and then. Alcohol notwithstanding, it probably wasn't a cocktail party in that apartment, with Katharine Hepburn and Cary Grant in a scintillating quipping match. More like a rabid wolverine and its mate.

The remainder of the afternoon unfolded like a play, or a movie—a rather depressing movie, I should think. Along the lines of Bergman, but artless. There does exist a faux cinema verité film of Ginsberg and his pals from 1957, which is not half bad, titled *Pull My Daisy*, shot by the estimable photographer Robert Frank and "produced" by the then abstract expressionist painter Alfred Leslie. It's now nearly impossible to get hold of, due to litigation between Frank and Leslie.

The film is loosely based on the third act of a play Kerouac wrote, originally titled *The Beat Generation*. Kerouac doesn't appear in the film but delivers a voice-over narration. The whole thing has an improvisational feel to it, much of it successful, or at least amusing. Ginsberg, Corso, and Orlovsky, essentially, are playing themselves. The plot is flimsy, but the antics of the youthful Ginsberg and his friends, including the painter Larry Rivers playing the Kerouac character, have a merry, almost Dada feel. I somehow don't think Tristan Tzara, Hugo Ball, and Kurt Schwitters were in the minds of the author and players, but no matter. The rather dour Swiss-born Robert Frank (best known for his realist photographs that make up *The Americans*) had a fascination with the Beats, in many respects his opposite, at least temperamentally. Regardless, his original camerawork and direction pull the film together and provide a rhythm to all the shenanigans. The memory of Allen's apartment that afternoon would strike me forever after as the ruins of *Pull My Daisy*.

■

I don't remember the exact sequence of phone calls and events after we returned from lunch. Nor the specifics of our conversation, apart from Allen introducing me to a form of the blues, the one-stringed slide guitar—in this instance, judging by the record sleeve, played by a derelict-looking older black man on a street corner in L.A. Allen taught a course on the blues at Brooklyn College and seemed to have a real feeling for the music. I half suspect all his dopey chanting, the tiny cymbals and childish songs (meant, I guess, to be in the spirit of Blake), was a surrogate, his way of singing the blues. I found it embarrassing, perhaps at moments endearing. We certainly didn't discuss poetry.

But not long after we got back, the phone began ringing. I seem to remember Orlovsky screaming and pounding next door, but that soon blended into the ambient noise. Perhaps the first call was the one from Cape Breton Island, the northeastern part of Nova Scotia. I had to piece bits together, but on the other end of the line was a former director of the Naropa Institute— one of the shady ersatz swamis associated with the place who hadn't worked out too well and somewhere along the line had contracted AIDS, of which he was now dying.

It was a one-way conversation for the most part, Allen throughout making periodic thoughtful-sounding grunts and acknowledgments. This went on for quite some time. The man on the other end was almost certainly hysterical, probably screaming something like, "I'm going to fucking DIE, dammit," or so I interpreted from the expression on Allen's face. Allen listened, nodding, grunting, patient for a long while, until finally, cutting short the conversation, he said, "Well, what we've got here is a real koan, don't we?" A koan is, approximately, an insoluble Zen riddle, a metaphysical puzzle with no answer. This is not how I would have characterized his friend's dilemma. It left the poor man out of his mind with frustration, rage, and disbelief, not that there was anything helpful Allen could really have said. The conversation was concluded. Allen's Buddhism, I surmised, served him as a handy tool for any number of awkward occasions.

Allen did not seem in any way upset by this conversation, and we quickly settled back into our own desultory exchange. I do recall Allen was inquisitive and I was forthcoming. That was probably the conversational dynamic. I enjoyed the frankness of the to-and-fro. He was among the sharpest people I have met in my life. A legendary self-mythologizer and bullshitter, he had no appetite for a second-rate performance from the likes of me. He always cut to the chase, old Allen did.

The next phone call involved the Barry Miles biography of Allen, due out later that year. Allen wanted some further changes. The fellow on the other end was not obliging him. Mistakes had gone uncorrected, Allen insisted. There was still time, Allen insisted. This went on for quite a bit. Allen didn't raise his voice, but he was mildly bullying, there was a hint of threat. The conversation ended unsatisfactorily.

Allen was left agitated and muttering. Can you imagine someone writing a biography about you? Even someone admiring with the best intentions, even someone gullible enough to buy ninety-five percent of your self-justifying bullshit, even someone intent on producing a hagiography disguised as a biography? What if the author inadvertently told the truth about you here and there? Oh, the horror, the humiliation . . . With his appetite for fame, as with so much else, Allen introduced discomfort and distress in his life. He had brought this down on himself.

The phone almost immediately began ringing again. "I'm sorry," Allen said to me, picking up the receiver. He was suddenly very alert, in a way I hadn't witnessed before: all the lights switched on in a most impressive fashion. It was a young man he'd been seeing, a boy, actually, fifteen or sixteen, calling Allen from a pay phone at the Jersey City Medical Center. The kid had slipped away from his parents—while they were all, presumably, visiting a sick relation—and was making this surreptitious love call. Had to talk to Allen, see him, etc. You know the drill.

Allen was beside himself, in a terrible panic. "Yes, yes, but we mustn't talk now, yes, yes, of course, but . . ." The call didn't last long, but Allen was really knocked off his pins and set to gibbering. I don't doubt for a moment that the FBI had kept Allen in its sights over the years. He had long been denouncing the government, the military-industrial complex, U.S. foreign policy, corporate America, what have you, all in a rather simplistic but generally accurate fashion. At the same time, he had been championing gay sex, free love, pot smoking, free speech, free this, free that, long before any of these things were fashionable. In fact, while it was dangerous to do so. Allen had been among the first, and most prominent, to accuse the CIA of being involved in the heroin trade in Indochina, during the Vietnam War and afterward.

No question the FBI kept track of Allen, and may well have tapped his line. But he had a rather elaborate paranoid fantasy about the sort of resources it was devoting to nailing him on a morals charge—presumably sex with a minor. The FBI had been monitoring his every move, every conversation, for over forty years, toying with him, torturing him. The trap could snap shut at any moment. And there he'd be—an American Oscar Wilde, without the drolleries.

I tried to be comforting. The FBI does hound and ruin innocent people. In fact, they do so routinely. But if they had been intent on catching Allen with an underage boy, among other things, surely they would have done so years before. Stupid and inefficient an organization though they are, had they chosen to put Allen out of business, so to speak, he'd be out of business.

But Allen seemed to enjoy indulging himself with his assorted obsessions. I found them rather curious, diverting even, but this was my first time through. In the long term, since his obsessions didn't change or go away, I should think they became tedious. Another of Allen's obsessions that he chose to share in the course of our afternoon was Norman Podhoretz—the right-wing public intellectual and author of several repugnant books, including *Making It*. Apparently they had been having at one another since they were both students at Columbia. Podhoretz had been baiting Allen and his beatnik writer friends for decades, as enemies of decency and normalcy and civilized behavior, etc. Why Allen bothered with this noisome creature, editor of *Commentary* for thirty-five years and apologist for every U.S. government predation at home and abroad, is beyond me, though not at all out of character for Allen. He talks about his obsession with Podhoretz in an interview:

> Gee, Good old Norman . . . If he weren't there like a wall I can butt my head against, I wouldn't have anybody to hate. And why hate him? He's part of my world, and he's sort of like the character . . . the Blue Meanie . . . But did I ever really hate him, or was I just sort of fascinated by him? . . . I saw him as a sacred personage in my life, in a way; someone whose vision is so opposite from mine that it's provocative and interesting . . .

But it was more than that for Allen. He'd dream of Podhoretz, write letters in his head to him all the time, perhaps even sending a few. He was fascinated with Podhoretz, but maybe not so much as he was fascinated by his obsession with Podhoretz, about which he could go on at great length without any special prompting. Carrying on about Podhoretz seemed to soothe Allen, perhaps like an extended version of one of the mantras he liked to chant.

Then the phone rang again. Allen stiffened, anxious that it was the boy, but this time it was his old sidekick Gregory Corso. This was familiar territory but not particularly welcome. Corso needed money, fast, presumably for heroin. He would be by directly.

The buzzer rang not long after and presently a breathless Corso appeared—thirty-five years older than the *Pull My Daisy* version, grizzled, ravaged, but still very much the same guy, the picture of the street punk turned sixty-something. Corso was in no mood for chitchat. He had "friends" waiting in a car downstairs. He needed money and he needed it quick. Corso and Allen had a brief quarrel in the next room, and Allen, like an exasperated, indulgent parent, quickly capitulated and went off to write Corso a check. This was clearly an old routine between them. "Talk to August Kleinzahler here while I take care of this. He's an interesting poet."

I smiled at Corso, trying out my best *friendly, deferential* smile. It's not that I wasn't excited to meet him. I'd walked through not a few cities as a youngster with his book of poems *Gasoline* in my pocket: New Orleans, El Paso, Mexico City, Santa Barbara. I was certainly keener to meet Gregory than I would have been to meet, say, Allen Tate. Or Edith Sitwell. But I'd long ago stopped reading him with any pleasure, and he'd long ago given up writing anything of interest.

Corso looked my way briefly, registered mild contempt, and shouted for Allen to "fucking hurry up." Allen grumbled something from the other room, where he was fastidiously entering the amount of the check into his checkbook and tearing off the check. He walked back into the room with a sigh and a most unconvincing minatory glare.

Corso was gone like he'd received the baton in the last leg of a relay race. No thank you. No good-bye. Junkies really are so one-dimensional, don't you find?

Allen wasn't terribly put out by any of this. Their interaction was of a familial nature. "Did you and Gregory have a chance to talk?" Allen asked solicitously. "No, not really," I said. The room in which we'd been chatting had grown noticeably darker. Evening was on its way. "You don't have to go just yet, do you?" Allen asked. "Soon," I said. He looked and sounded a bit needy. I think that's when he remembered it was Burroughs's birthday. I haven't a clue what reminded him, but off he went again in a great heat and presently had his friend on the other end of the line, solemnly conveying birthday greetings and promising gifts, an appropriate marking of the occasion, etc.

No sooner had Allen gotten off the phone and returned to chat than it rang again. This time it was a university in Pittsburgh. He was reluctant to go and read there but allowed his arm to be twisted and finally relented. "I'm trying to cut down on these things," he confessed gloomily. "Why don't you?" I said, in the tone of an affectionate but exasperated cousin, a tone that surprised me. "I can't help it. I can't stop."

Really it was time to go. I'd love to stay, really, but I've got to get back. It's been a gas. No, really. He struck me at that moment as more than just lonely. Of course, it was Sunday, and that depressing transitional part of winter afternoons, a time of day and year that would have been more easily handled in the countryside, or almost anywhere other than the East Village. It distressed me to leave him there by himself looking so unhappy.

Ginsberg called me up several months later in San Francisco and we got together, but it was the social, more public Ginsberg this time, even with only a handful of people around. This was a different Allen, rather manipulative, running operations, connecting this one with that one, all quite well-intentioned but a bit exhausting and irritating. He roped me into attending a Buddhist prayer ceremony in the basement of an AIDS hospice, not what I had in mind. But it was fine. A group of us went out to dinner at a Cuban restaurant. Philip Whalen was along, and he and Ginsberg sparred in the way that old friends sometimes do, none of the blows doing much damage. Whalen was grumpy but enjoying taking the piss out of Allen. We promised to keep in touch.

MUSIC XXVI

Spade Cooley beat his wife, Ella Mae, to death one evening in 1961 in front of their daughter. "You're going to watch me kill her," Spade told the girl. It seems Ella Mae had been going around town bragging that she had screwed Roy Rogers.

Actually, Spade Cooley and Roy Rogers were good buddies, and Spade owed much of his fame and fortune to Roy, chiefly on account of their very close resemblance to one another. Which, if she was telling the truth, might be regarded as a mitigating circumstance for Ella Mae's transgression, not to mention Spade's. The story goes that Spade was spotted outside the gate of Republic Pictures in 1937 and, because of his resemblance to Roy, began appearing as a stand-in for the singing cowboy. Pretty soon, Roy got a chance to hear Spade play the fiddle—and man, he could play that fiddle—and not long after that Spade Cooley was on his way.

Nothing was ever quite what it seemed about Cooley except that he was born in Grand, Oklahoma, in 1910, christened Donnell Cooley, and that Dad and Granddad were pretty able fiddlers themselves. As Spade would tell it later in life (when he was playing at the Redondo Pier in front of ten thousand fans), he was one-quarter Cherokee and had arrived in L.A. on a fast freight with a violin in hand and four cents in his pocket. He got his name by winning an extraordinary string of poker hands, at least that's what he claimed.

However it all came to pass, by 1942 Spade Cooley was a star of stage, radio, and film. By that point the ballroom of the Venice Pier had become Spade's home base, where he played for up to four thousand dancing fans every Saturday night. By 1943 there were dance halls all over California, some huge, some tiny. So much money was to be made that even the legendary Texan Bob Wills, along with his Texas Playboys, moved his base of operations west. This initially created a problem for Spade when Bert Phillips, who had originally opened the big Venice Pier Ballroom to cater to local GIs, dumped Spade in favor of Wills and the Playboys. Spade didn't think much of this, not one bit, and insisted that Phillips put on a weekend-long "Battle of the Bands" between Spade Cooley's outfit and Wills's. Spade, remarkably, carried the day. I say "remarkably" because Wills and his Boys more or less invented the genre of Western swing and were pretty dang good at it, too. Maybe a bit of Golden State chauvinism was at work there, who knows? Maybe Bob and the Playboys had gotten a little too deep into the fun the night before. One can only speculate about such things in the lively arts or wind up taking the word of some superannuated grip or girlfriend thirty years after the fact.

What we do know for certain is that Cooley moved his show down to the Riverside Ballroom and made a killing as the *new* "King of Western Swing." In September 1943, Cooley signed with OKeh Records and in '44 made his first screen appearance in Bing Crosby's *Singing Sheriff.* In 1945, Spade signed with Columbia and recorded his greatest hit, "Shame on You." The following year he married his second wife, Ella Mae, and was also arrested and acquitted on a rape charge. His daughter, Melody, who was forced to watch the murder of her mother and whose testimony later served to convict her father, was born in 1947.

Spade got into television in the early '50s with *The Spade Cooley Show*, winning local Emmy Awards in 1952 and '53. However, the success of the new *Lawrence Welk Show* finally drove him out of television in 1958, at which point Spade decided to build a recreational park in the Mojave Desert called Water Wonderland that was to consist of a series of artificial lakes. The actual digging would have begun that year had the project not collapsed for want of sense. You've got to love Spade Cooley, even if you never heard him play the fiddle.

But you'd be missing something good. Western swing is a genre of country music that became popular between the '30s and '50s, when jazz swing orchestras were the rage. The countrified version takes on a number of the characteristics of the jazz model, with large bands and syncopated dance-oriented rhythms. And if Western swing sounds like a hybrid or mongrelized genre, bear in mind so is country music itself, and so is jazz, the latter an amalgam of field hollers, marches, rags, European song forms, West African polyrhythms, and Caribbean stylings, among other elements.

In Western swing, depending on the band, or the vintage of

any given band, one hears elements of black rural blues, mariachi music, jazz, reels, rags, polkas, schottisches, breakdowns, two-steps, and even a Texas-flavored waltz or two—whatever passed through town. One forgets how many immigrants were living in Texas in the early twentieth century at the inception of dance hall music's popularity.

Spade Cooley's band would occasionally swell up to twenty-five pieces, as it did with Decca in 1950 when he added a string section. As interest in cowboy singers and Western swing bands with fancy arrangements began to fade in the late '40s, Cooley introduced horns and cut back on the country, but with the result that his label, RCA, kicked Cooley off the hillbilly roster and moved him into the pop lineup.

The sides on Columbia between 1943 and '46 catch Spade Cooley at the peak of his powers. He was a swinging fiddler; his daddy taught him that. His band of this era features three fiddles, including Cooley, two guitars, a bassist, drummer, two accordionists, a harpist, two steel guitars, and Tex Williams on vocals. Williams is an okay vocalist, but it's on the instrumental pieces that the music really stands out. I remember the first time I heard Cooley in a little used-record shop and immediately asked the clerk, "Who's that?"

Three days after beating and stomping and burning and strangling his wife Ella Mae to death in front of fourteen-year-old Melody, under arrest and awaiting trial, Spade Cooley suffered a heart attack, not his first. Shortly thereafter, on the heels of the highly publicized and lurid spectacle of a trial, Spade dropped his insanity plea. Regardless, the jury found him insane and he was sent to Vacaville Medical Center, a prison/hospital facility. A model prisoner, Spade Cooley was granted parole in 1969, a little over eight years after murdering Ella Mae. He was to be released eight months later, in February 1970, but that November the prison authorities granted him a seventy-two-hour leave to perform a benefit for the Alameda County Sheriff's Association. Cooley received a standing ovation on completing his first public appearance in over a decade, walked offstage, and dropped dead.

LUCIA BERLIN

Lucia Berlin was a Western writer, by which I do not mean a genre writer of cowboy tales like Zane Grey or the younger Elmore Leonard, but that her stories, with only a few exceptions, are situated west of the Great Plains or in Mexico. Berlin herself was born in Alaska and spent most of her childhood in Chile— a setting for several stories. The daughter of a mining man, she also lived in Montana, Idaho, Arizona, and Texas. El Paso is revisited time and again in her writing. The majority of her adult life was spent in New Mexico, Mexico, and the San Francisco Bay Area, chiefly Oakland.

The American West is on a different scale from the East. With Lucia Berlin we are very far away from the parlors of Boston and New York, and quite far away, too, from the fiction of manners, unless we are speaking of very bad manners. Landscape rules in the West. The individual is diminished or obliterated, along with his or her personality and will:

> It was cool and smelled like the ocean. A few times the fog lifted and we saw stars. The best part was when the huge Japanese ships filled with cars came up the estuary. Like moving skyscrapers, all lit up. Ghost ships gliding past not making a sound. The waves they made were so big they were silent,

rolling, not splashing. There were never more than one or two figures on any of the decks. Men alone, smoking, looking out at the city with no expression at all.

The principal narrator in this story is a woman in early middle age who is having an intense and troubled affair with one of her son's teenage friends. At this point, the two of them are trespassing on a sailing boat in the local marina, drinking, making love, and taking in the evening's sights and sounds.

In "Here It Is Saturday," the narrator is a young white male en route from the city to the county jail:

> After a long climb you come upon a valley in the hills. The land used to be the summer estate of a millionaire called Spreckles. The fields around the county jail are like the grounds of a French castle. That day there were a hundred Japanese plum trees in bloom. Flowering quince. Later on there were fields of daffodils, then iris.
>
> In front of the jail is a meadow where there is a herd of buffalo. About sixty buffalo. Already there were six new calves. For some reason all the sick buffalo in the U.S. get sent here. Veterinarians treat them and study them. You can tell when dudes on the bus are doing their first time because they all freak out. "Whoa! What the fuck! Do they feed us buffalo? . . ."
>
> The prison and the women's jail, the auto shop and the greenhouses. No people, no other houses, so it seems as if you're suddenly in an ancient prairie lit by sunbeams in the

mist. The Bluebird bus always frightens the buffalo even though it comes once a week. They break into a gallop, stampede off toward the green hills.

Both passages have an element of the surreal, reflecting what happens when man-made instances of gigantism or extreme displacement intrude on the natural landscape. And both suggest how distant Berlin's work is from the conventions of contemporary fiction with its emphasis on the domestic. Her stories are radically undomesticated, in both character and subject matter. There is no equilibrium, only disarray; behavior, on the whole, is feral.

Berlin's style is unadorned, often telegraphic, rough-hewn, as if it were modeled on speech, the intimate letter, and the journal. At its best, her writing has an uncommon transparency, so that we are almost wholly unaware of any authorial presence. Readers looking for resemblances to more familiar contemporary American fiction might well seize on Raymond Carver. At the most superficial level, the titles of their books have a similar poker-faced offhandedness that counterpoints the gravity and bleakness of their subject matter. Carver: *Will You Please Be Quiet, Please?* or *Where I'm Calling From*; Berlin: *Where I Live Now* or *So Long*. Their protagonists tend to be blue-collar, though Berlin's are often better educated and more exotic, as well as being psychologically nearer the edge. Like Carver, Berlin spent most of her adult life working in menial jobs while raising a family and knows that world intimately. Drink figures prominently in both writers' work. Both are Westerners who situate their stories in the West, though for Carver locale has nothing like the significance it has for Berlin. Both use a bare-boned, demotic prose. They are dark writers: character, truth, destiny, what have you are revealed through desperation and failure.

Carver is the more polished writer, however. His achievement lies in his facility with voice and in the novelty of an art given over to the lives of the ordinary and flawed, who are portrayed in handsomely carpentered stories and well-judged prose. He is part of an American Realist tradition that runs from Dreiser and Crane, the Hemingway of the Nick Adams stories, Steinbeck, Farrell, and Algren. Berlin is both inside and outside this tradition. She is a wilder writer than Carver, with a greater stylistic range and a wider repertoire of voice and subject matter. Carver's stories haven't the brutality of Berlin's. Few stories do. But, in the end, for all his enormous skills, he is a mannered writer, one story very like the next.

The unevenness of Berlin's stories is in the service, I think, of her larger project. One story can be almost slovenly in execution, while the next has the controlled grace of a writer like Mavis Gallant: Berlin is several writers, some raw, some cooked. But more often than not the delivery is stripped down and usually in the first person. Details of character and place are so vivid that the stories feel autobiographical, an impression reinforced by her habit of going back to the same places—Oakland, Mexico, Albuquerque, El Paso—and characters: mother; the husband who's a junkie; the other who's a jazz musician; the sister; the sister dying; the boy lover.

The literary model is Chekhov, but there are extraliterary models, too, including the extended jazz solo, with its surges, convolutions, and asides. But Berlin's aim is Chekhov's: "truth, unconditional and honest." The writer must strive to be as objective as the chemist, as concealed as the puppeteer, to resist manipulating character and complicating situation for the designs of plot and resolution.

The story "Carmen" is characteristic of Berlin's work. It begins in Albuquerque, continues in El Paso and Juarez, and returns to Albuquerque. The narrator, Mona, a pregnant American, is asked by her heroin-addict husband to travel to Juarez, via El Paso, which is on the Mexican border, to score some heroin.

> It was still hot in El Paso. I walked across the sinking soft tarmac from the plane, smelling the dirt and sage I remembered from childhood. I told the cabdriver to take me to the bridge, but first to drive around the alligator pond.
>
> "Alligators? Them old alligators died off years ago."

Mona crosses the bridge into Juarez.

> It was hard climbing the stairs to the fourth floor. I was big with the baby and my legs were swollen and sore. I caught my breath in sobs at each landing. My knees and hands were shaking. I knocked on the door of number 43. Mel opened it and I stumbled in.

"Hey, sweetheart, what's happening?"

"Water, please." I sat on a dirty vinyl sofa. He brought me a Diet Coke, wiped the top with his shirt, smiled. He was dirty, handsome, moved like a cheetah . . .

"Where is La Nacha?" The woman was never referred to just as Nacha. "The Nacha," whatever that meant. She came in, dressed in a black man's suit and a white shirt. She sat at a chair behind the desk. I couldn't tell if she was a male transvestite or a woman trying to look like a man. She was dark, almost black, with a Mayan face, red-black lipstick and nail polish, dark glasses. Her hair was short, slick. She held a stubby hand out to Mel without looking at me. I handed him the money. I saw her count the money.

Mona has been instructed to put the heroin in a condom inside her vagina. Her husband, Noodles, also told her not to let Mel out of her sight, not even for a minute. But at one point Mona has to urinate and briefly leaves the room.

When I got back I remembered that I wasn't supposed to leave Mel alone. He was smiling. He handed me the condom, rolled up into a ball.

"Here you go, precious, you have a good trip. Go on now, put it away, like a good girl." I turned around and acted like I was shoving it inside myself but it was just inside my too-tight underpants. Outside, in the dark of the hall I moved it to my bra.

I took the steps slowly, like a drunk. It was dark, filthy.

At the second landing I heard the door open downstairs,

noises from the street. Two young boys ran up the stairs. *"Fí-jate no más!"* One of them pinned me to the wall, the other got my purse. Nothing was in it but loose bills, makeup. Everything else was in a pocket inside my jacket. He hit me.

"Let's fuck her," the other one said.

"How? You need a dick four feet long."

"Turn her around, *bato*."

Just as he hit me again a door opened and an old man came running down the stairs with a knife. The boys turned and ran back outside. "Are you well?" the man asked in English.

Mona flies back to Albuquerque and goes straight from the airport to the trailer where her husband has been waiting for her.

He sat on the edge of the bed. On the table his outfit was ready and waiting. "Let me see it." I handed him the balloon. He opened the cupboard above the bed and put it on the tiny scale. He turned and slapped me hard across the face. He had never hit me before. I sat there, numb, next to him. "You left Mel alone with it. Didn't you. Didn't you."

But Berlin's range was wide. "Evening in Paradise," for example, is a gorgeous story set in Puerta Vallarta during the filming of *The Night of the Iguana*, with some inspired bits of Ava Gardner in it. And then there are the Mother stories, which appear throughout Berlin's collections, and often show the writer at her best. These revolve around a manipulative, alcoholic, rather sadistic character who manages at times to be quite endearing and droll in a Bette Davis, damn-the-torpedoes sort of way. You are not likely to forget Mother. And then the delicate love story "Romance" takes place in upper Manhattan and involves two fortyish professionals. It is told in such a different register that it might have been written by another author—the aforementioned Ms. Gallant, for example.

Yet the writer Lucia Berlin most puts me in mind of is Richard Yates, better known as a novelist, but also the author of two remarkable collections of short stories: *Eleven Kinds of Loneliness* and *Liars in Love*. Yates's technique is a good deal more familiar, and his writing more polished, or cooked, than Berlin's. He was an Easterner, a New Yorker and Bostonian, who found a New York trade publisher and some success early in his career. Like Berlin, however, he believed in the Chekhovian notion that a writer's business is to describe a situation so thoroughly that the reader can no longer evade it. Both have stock characters who become bleakly familiar over the course of their work. Both write about alcoholism, not in the Cheever manner of cocktail-party drinking drifting out of hand toward hallucination and divorce, but the sort that ends up in psychiatric wards. And both writers are relentless, on occasion horribly so: when you are several paragraphs into a story you get a sinking, even sickening, feeling of recognition. But you read on. It is writing of a very high order and not always easy to take.

CLOSING IT DOWN

ON THE PALISADES

The streets, lawns, roofs, pavement—everything is matted with leaves, oak and maple for the most part, beech as well. I find it rather intoxicating, not least because San Francisco, where I've lived for nearly thirty years, doesn't have a proper autumn, at least not as an Easterner like myself thinks of it. But also because this time of year here on the Palisades is the one I most associate with childhood: rain, leaves, Halloween pumpkins, galoshes, the smell of the coat closet at the back of class, wet wool and shiny slickers, the last days of recess outside in the playground, before the onset of cold, the going back of the clocks and, along with that, darkness, the lit rooms and closed curtains of winter.

The world through these windows, where I've registered the seasons and much else over the course of sixty years, will soon recede into memory. In a couple of days I'll sit down in a small, noisy, cluttered room with lawyers, the realtor, my sister and brother-in-law, and hand the keys to this house over to a very pleasant young Chinese couple who will begin their own lives together here. They are very excited.

I am not. I like it here. This is home, even if I haven't really lived here for forty-two years, my psychological redoubt: red-brick, slate-roofed, sitting on a five-hundred-foot basalt sill that reaches down to the "lordly Hudson." It is what is most solid about me and what has allowed me to live the sort of life one might not associate with any notion of solidity. This is who I am, what I'm from. And with the sale of the house goes my connection to this place. I am untethered.

I turned up in New Jersey at the beginning of August, a couple of weeks after my sister and I had decided to keep our mother in the nursing home where she was rehabilitating after another bad fall, wheelchair-bound and suffering from senile dementia. The weather was sultry, the kind of weather I'm not used to anymore. San Francisco has a cool climate, especially in summer. But it was beautiful here in the very early morning, around dawn, with the sparrows, wrens, and robins all darting around, diving into the shrubs, clustering on branches, squeezing into cracks under the eaves of the garage, singing up a storm. The house has a screened-in back porch overlooking the yard. It's a lovely yard; less so these days, with a couple of McMansions crowding the eastern and northern prospects, but still the nicest thing about the house, and probably what made it so appealing to buyers. By eight thirty or nine, the power mowers, tree "surgeons," and cicadas make for a most unpastoral din, which lasts until dusk, when the birds return, then the fireflies. Sometimes wild turkeys and the occasional deer pass unexpectedly through the yard.

The house, and much of the rest of the Palisades section of Fort Lee, was built around 1925, at a time when the garden city movement was under way in Britain, and, independently, Frederick Law Olmsted and Clarence Stein's garden suburb movement was taking hold in America. This neighborhood, across the Hudson from uptown Manhattan, about a mile south of the George Washington Bridge on the Jersey side, has lost more than a little of its character and charm over the years with the proliferation of McMansions—what my father used to call "Greco-Roman fortresses" or "mausolea"—which take up entire quarter-acre lots. But when I was growing up it was an uncommonly lovely place by American standards: not Hampstead, to be sure, but a lot closer to it than to later suburban horrors like Levittown. There was a good deal of variety in the architecture: Georgian, like our house, Federal, Tudor, Norman French, Gothic, Mission, all revival, all bastardized, but not outlandish or gross. When I was a child, a large amusement park bordered the southern edge of the town until it was replaced by high-rise condominiums in the 1970s; a narrow half-mile swathe of woodland overlooked the Hudson to the north before the area was developed in the 1960s. Nowadays, the population of Fort Lee is about thirty-seven thousand, twice what it was then, mostly condominium dwellers, nearly half of them Asian, principally Korean. There are also quite a few Russians. When I was young, the town was almost exclusively Italian, first- and second-generation southern Italian. It was a good deal sleepier, less full of traffic, and, after school and at weekends, children played in the street. Children are nowhere to be seen these days. Nor are their parents, who go to and from their homes in sleek SUVs with clouded windows. The only people you see on the streets are domestics, pushing prams or walking dogs, and gardeners, Mexican and Central American. It's a much wealthier neighborhood than it was, and the wealth is on display.

A young married couple with two small children sixty-three years ago, living in a not very glamorous apartment in Weehawken, a few towns south, my parents were out looking for houses in the area one weekend when they saw 83 Bluff for sale. As my father used to tell the story, my mother immediately lit up and told him, "That's the one." The owner, a commercial artist, was apparently reluctant to sell. I know exactly where he was coming from. "It was perfect," my father liked to say, meaning close to Manhattan and just far enough away from my mother's family in Jersey City. He paid seventeen thousand dollars. His own parents, also in Jersey City, considered the expense wildly profligate, and let my father know.

"It smells like a sewer in here." This was not helpful. But my older sister wasn't entirely wrong. Our elderly parents, one dead six years, had wasted away in this house. But my sister's tone of voice suggested it was somehow my fault, or that I had brought the sewer smell with me from San Francisco. My sister and her husband, the bank examiner, come by every Sunday to harrumph around the house for half an hour, grab a handful of my mother's dresses for charity, and go to Hiram's for a hot dog. My brother-in-law, who likes to remind you he has an MBA from

Harvard, stands in the background, arms folded, and offers counsel, usually in the form of: "Augie, if I were you . . ." or "You know what you *should* do." This isn't helpful either.

My sister, eight and a half years my senior, loves me. But she thinks me feckless and disturbed. She's right: I am disturbed, though hardly in the way she means. She is a psychiatric social worker and thinks most people, especially members of her family, are "disturbed" in varying degrees. What was disturbing me at that moment was how the hell I was going to get all this shit out of the house by the September 28 closing date. It woke me up in a panic at three a.m. night after night. By "feckless" (a word my father might have used, rather than my sister), she means I didn't graduate from an Ivy League school (she went to Smith); I'm not married (anymore); I have not raised a family, nor do I have plans to in the immediate future (see *not married*); I don't own a house (lifelong renter) or even a car; and I don't have a job (belletrist). If a sensible, attractive, middle-aged lady came across me on a dating Web site she would immediately think to herself: feckless, disturbed. Also, loser.

The panic about clearing out the house wasn't the only thing keeping me up. I had a dread of losing the place—a very real, primal dread in the pit of my stomach. It would have been nice to have someone to hold on to at three in the morning, but it would be too much to ask another person to participate in a three-month ordeal at the Mortality Motel, especially with all the memory-driven emotional weather blowing through.

There is, however, one woman in my life: Argia Rubino (née

Argia di Meglio, seventy-eight years ago in Ischia). She and her late husband, Sal, were our next-door neighbors for more than forty years. Sal was terrific, too, a small, tightly wound, chain-smoking dynamo. We got friendly in the late 1980s and early 1990s when I used to house-sit for my parents during the month of February and he'd come by for a cup of coffee and to chat. I've never seen—even in cartoons—someone of that age and stature, not to mention the chain-smoking, shovel snow the way Sal did. Nowadays it would be on YouTube. He was a great talker: funny, opinionated, profane; Argia talks up a storm as well. Their son, who comes by now and then to pick up his own small son, whom Argia often has in tow, seems pretty taciturn. How would it be otherwise?

After Sal died and, not long after him, my father, Argia, and my mother would go out to dinner now and then, which is how I got to know her. She's direct and can be pugnacious with those who make her *agitata*, but she has an abundant sweetness and vulnerability and I trust her utterly. She can be hard as nails, too, and just as sharp. She's an old-fashioned Washington Heights girl, after all, who arrived in the U.S. at the age of five with the rest of her family to join her father in a small cold-water flat, all five of them. Her father lived with Argia in his old age. He worked in the garden all day, and the only time he ever acknowledged me was one day when a friend and I were laying some concrete at the foot of the back steps. He just stood and shook his head.

When my sister complained about the state of the place, it

was Argia who hooked me up with Super Dario, the removalist. Dario owed her. Argia had got him a pile of work cleaning houses and apartments after he arrived here from Colombia, where he trained as an engineer. He doesn't do cleaning work anymore, except for a few clients he's had for years. But for Argia he'll drop everything.

Dario came to clean the house the weekend before Argia began showing it. He brought his sister-in-law along to help. It was quite a performance, and the smell of disinfectants, floor wax, and the rest would have knocked a hippo sideways. The house hadn't been properly cleaned in years. Bill, the longtime cleaner, would roar around for ninety minutes with his vacuum, steal what he could get away with, and go off to the next job. When the stealing got out of hand, we let him go and my mother's caregivers would clean up a bit when they had a chance. They didn't do much.

Even my sister was impressed. "It doesn't smell as bad as it did," she volunteered. Dario is a smallish man of slight build, somewhere in his early forties, I'd guess: bright, sweet-natured, very much the churchgoing, devoted family man. He's also as strong as a 220-pound linebacker. After Dario and his sister-in-law were done, Dario looked at me speculatively, not without pity, and announced, "Au-GEE, I thinks you need help getting rid of." In short order the garage was full of miscellaneous junk and I was hauling out two cans and ten black plastic garbage bags every Tuesday and Friday night for the garbagemen, and two big pieces of furniture every Friday: the town would pick up two "large pieces" on Saturdays. Dario referred to small pieces of furniture as "Mexican sandwiches." "You put out, they disappear. No you worry. They take."

Why, the reader experienced in such matters will ask, didn't I simply have an estate sale? There are the mundane excuses: my sister wanted this and that, or maybe she didn't, she'd discuss it with her husband; at one point I seriously considered taking an apartment nearby and would have wanted some of the furniture and crockery, pots, pans, whatnot; and of the few pieces of furniture of any value, the buyers wanted the big Victorian cabinet in the living room along with the dining-room table and chairs. But the truth is that I was reluctant, viscerally, psychologically, to let any of it go; and I didn't want strangers traipsing through our house, looking appraisingly at this or that, dismissing it as worthless or, worse, walking out with it.

The furnishings haven't really changed since I was a child. This is what a living room should look like, our living room. These are the sorts of dishes one eats one's dinner from. That's where those paintings belong, right on that wall over there, where they've been for fifty years. Even my childhood bedroom hasn't changed much. The wallpaper is less bright, but the dresser, bookcase, and desk have been there forever. I can show you the photographs. I dislike change, at least as it relates to childhood memory. I still haven't visited the new Museum of Modern Art in New York. I would be brokenhearted if the big Henri Rousseau painting *The Sleeping Gypsy* were no longer on the wall in the lobby as one walked past the ticket booth. It hasn't been there for years. But it should be there. Everything should be where it's supposed to be, which is where it was; if you remove one significant element, everything collapses. Much as a body would, if you removed a thighbone or major organ. It all goes cattywampus. *All the king's horses and all the king's men* . . . The house, in some queer way, has become part of my body, or an extension of it. And as the rooms are laid out and furnished, with the mirror above the dresser there, and the desk with the Chinese lamp by the living-room window over there, so is my imagination and my way of taking in the world ordered, a cockamamie variant of Matteo Ricci's Memory Palace.

I was not very pleased when Argia began bringing other realtors and prospective buyers into the house. Of course, this was how one went about selling a house, and we were all agreed on the sale of the house, the sooner the better. My mother's nursing home care was grotesquely expensive. I couldn't handle the costs of living in the house myself, even had my sister decided to relinquish her share of the place and hand it over to me outright, debts be damned, we'll figure all that out somehow down the road. Property taxes, utility bills, upkeep on an old house . . . no way. Suck it up. Let's get this show on the road. You've got a life to lead in San Francisco.

Easy for you to say. The other realtors, mostly older women, were an odd, creepy lot. They were at once casual and cheery— thought we'd just stop by and say hello—and unabashedly wolfish and mercenary. They were also rather sneering: what a

curious old dump filled up to the brim with tchotchkes, un-
speakable furniture. The wall over there would need to be removed, that one, too. No, that wouldn't work. What sort of
people lived in a place like this? Another era, I suppose. And
the kitchen . . . A builder might want it for the land . . . And
there I'd be, in the shadows, where Argia had positioned me,
looking and feeling like an underutilized docent or the aged
family mooncalf.

I wound up clearing the house out in as torturous a manner
as possible, room by room, drawer by drawer, with Argia coming
by twice a day to urge me on, and Dario, who had at least three
other jobs and a wife in and out of the hospital, showing up
when he could at weekends to help me with the heavier things.
"Au-GEE," he said cheerfully one Sunday evening after four
hours of removalizing, my back and knees aching, "we're nut
even halfways through, hee hee."

It wasn't going nearly fast enough. I was at it from before
dawn—couldn't sleep—till dusk. It felt as though I were cleaning the Augie-an stables. Argia was anxious. Dario was anxious.
My sister began complaining less, coming round more often,
staying longer and taking more. My brother-in-law appeared
one morning with a couple of movers and took away a few desks
and bureaus he and my sister fancied for their own house. I
called the Salvation Army, who sent round two extra-jumbo
dimmies who didn't want to take anything, even for free. "That's
an early-nineteenth-century French antique sofa, classical revival," I protested. "A dealer could probably sell that for four

grand!" "Too old," they said. I wound up having to give them a C-note to haul off six big, perfectly useful pieces of furniture.

The closing was delayed. Heaven. Then delayed again. There were problems securing a mortgage. The black plastic bags continued to fill up. I came across one big box in the attic filled with my publications, press clippings, awards, which my parents, unknown to me, had saved. One day I went through my mother's desk drawers. Photographs, hundreds and hundreds. Too much to bear. I'd resolved early on, while cleaning the attic and finding other old photographs, that if this was going to get done, I'd be obliged, like Lot on his retreat from Sodom and Gomorrah, to avert my eyes. But I couldn't help it: I had to separate the ones I wanted to keep and the ones I thought my sister would want. Scores of photographs I'd forgotten or never seen, tranches of memory that made me catch my breath. The one that really got to me was a large, professionally taken photo of my brother with his date at the high school senior prom, 1961, both of them looking so young, good-looking, and hopeful.

Another day, many days really, were devoted to going through my father's tchotchkes—small statues, figurines, odd bits of driftwood or stone he'd picked up—and, finally, throwing them into a trash bag. I might well have been with him when he chanced on these things, in junk shops, flea markets, or just lying there on the ground: his treasures. This was what pleased him most in life, I think, hunting for these bits and pieces that he found intriguing for one reason or another. No, not for one reason or another: they were all lovely, all interesting; he had a wonderful eye. But they were of no value to anyone else, except perhaps to me, and I don't have room. My apartment in San Francisco is already crowded with my father's things. It's what's made returning here so much more bearable than I'd expected. My walls and shelves are covered with his masks, from Africa and Oceania, his bronze bodhisattvas, the old mortars and pestles he enjoyed collecting. But there I was, sitting on the back porch in his favorite armchair, the one he read and napped in, or enjoyed an Old Grand-Dad on the rocks in, his absolute favorite spot—sitting there and throwing out, one by one, the things he loved having near him, to look at or pick up and roll around in his hand.

I went to see my mother in the nursing home. It was a Sunday. A perfect October morning, the foliage at its very best. Only a few days earlier I'd been caught in a shower of acorns as I walked along Abbott Boulevard. Farther along on my walk I came across a barberry shrub whose leaves were such a brilliant, fiery shade of red that it seemed unearthly. It turned out to be the winged euonymus, better known as the "burning bush." The seasons change so swiftly here, in comparison to out west. It is a pleasant drive to the nursing home, about forty-five minutes west-southwest. There's a good radio station from Columbia University, WKCR. It does country and bluegrass in that Sunday slot—first-rate.

My mother was slumped over in a wheelchair in the hallway, by herself, away from a cluster of other elderly people in wheelchairs by the central desk. A pleasant Filipina greeted me. I told her who I was and she took me over to my mother. I kneeled down. "Look who's here, Mrs. K." My mother, who'd been dozing, looked at me for a few seconds and then, on recognizing me, began shaking with sobs and nodding her head. I wheeled her to the room she shares with another woman, who wasn't there. A news show was on the TV, the talking heads sort, with a few retired generals and pundits having a back and forth about the Afghanistan war. My mother drifted in and out of sleep. I stroked her arm when she was awake, which made her smile. She'd deteriorated badly since I last saw her. I felt queasy. There was no meat on her at all, just bruised, veiny skin hanging off the bone. I tried to be gentle. At one point she told me her back hurt and asked me to get the attendant. The attendant came back to the room with me to give my mother some Percocet. My mother snarled at her like a cornered, half-dead bobcat. The attendant was used to this, sort of. I sat by her for a half an hour or so, listening to the "experts." "I've got to go now, Ma," I told her. She nodded. "I know, sweetheart."

The final pick-up came at five-thirty on Saturday morning. I'd already been awake for an hour or so, just lying there, thinking. The day before, Dario had helped me put the mattress and box spring out. The next day he gave the house its final clean and I moved to the Comfort Inn in Edgewater for the last two nights, leaving my mother's 1992 Oldsmobile Cutlass in the parking lot there for him to pick up, in exchange for all his work. It hardly seems fair, but he had coveted that car since I suggested maybe we could work something out. It has fewer than thirty thousand miles on it. "I likes old GMC cars. I used have '87 Electra. I fix." A few days after my return to San Francisco, he phoned me one morning to tell me all the plans he has for the car. He'd already bought two new tires. He wanted to know how I was doing.

That Saturday morning, as I lay there waiting, the house was empty and had been for a while, apart from my inflato-mattress and the furniture the buyers had bought. I rather liked it. It made me feel monkish. I live in such a clutter of books and *things* in San Francisco. I would be pleased to live like this, here, through the winter. I would be pleased simply to live here, simply. Or not simply. No one need know I'm here. I'd keep the lights off but for a small reading lamp. I could slip out to the twenty-four-hour A&P up by the high school in the middle of the night. I like twenty-four-hour supermarkets at three a.m. I like them more than museums. America is very good at that sort of thing.

■　■　■

ACKNOWLEDGMENTS

The author wishes to thank the *London Review of Books*,
where most of these essays first appeared, as well as its
editors, who improved the originals immeasurably in every
instance. The author also wishes to thank two brilliant and
recently made friends, Steve Emerson and Curtis Brown,
who also made significant improvements to the essays.
My thanks as well to my FSG editor, Jeremy M. Davies,
who's smart as paint and patient as . . . well, patient.

None of the above should be implicated
in the author's own limitations.

Printed in the USA
CPSIA information can be obtained
at www.ICGtesting.com
LVHW091137150724
785511LV00005B/381